How To Be Yourself

SIMPLE STRATEGIES TO BUILD CONFIDENCE, TRANSFORM YOUR MINDSET, BOOST SELF-ESTEEM, LOVE YOURSELF, IMPROVE YOUR HABITS AND CHANGE YOUR LIFE

Contents

Introduction _____ 9

Chapter 1: Love Yourself and Get Over Self-Hatred And Self-Loathing _____ 13

SELF-HATRED: WHY DON'T I LOVE MYSELF _____ 13
REDISCOVER YOUR REAL IDENTITY _____ 15
THOROUGHLY ANALYZING HOW MUCH YOU LOVE
   YOURSELF _____ 20
LEARNING TO LOVE YOURSELF _____ 22
   Observation _____ 23
   The Mirror Exercise _____ 23
   Being Present _____ 24
   Spending Fun Time _____ 25
   Communicate _____ 26
CLEAR YOUR MIND OF DESTRUCTIVE FEELINGS _____ 27
CONSIDER WHY YOU THINK SELF-LOVE IS IMPORTANT __ 28
THE IMPORTANCE OF RADICAL SELF-LOVE _____ 30

Chapter 2: Overcome Social Anxiety, Shyness, Self-Consciousness and Build Self-Esteem _____ 31

OVERCOMING SHYNESS AND SOCIAL ANXIETY _____ 31
   Start by Accepting and Acknowledging Your
     Fears _____ 32
   Changing Your Thought Patterns _____ 32
   Changing Your Focus _____ 33
   Love the Sound of Your Voice _____ 33
   Build a more practical and reasonable image of
     others _____ 33
   Tackle your inhibitions and fears _____ 34
   Have more faith in people _____ 34

Take risks to move outside your comfort zone ___ 35
Build your patience, courage, will-power, perseverance ___ 35
Build a more reasonable, practical and balanced picture of yourself ___ 36
Manage your breath to regulate emotional reactions ___ 36
Avoid negative thoughts ___ 37
Make daily reflection a habit ___ 38
Identify problems and fears, along with their triggers ___ 38
BUILDING SELF-ESTEEM ___ 39
Control your emotions ___ 39
Conquering Your Inner Critic ___ 40
Practice, Practice, Practice ___ 41
Using Affirmations to Change Your Thinking ___ 41
Changing Your Personal Narrative ___ 42
Change Your Mental Patterns ___ 42
Once Your Self-Esteem is Positive, You Project It Out ___ 43
Create an ideal self-image ___ 43
Reflect on your past ___ 44
Provide support for others ___ 45
FINDING SELF-ESTEEM WHEN YOU FEEL AT ODDS WITH YOURSELF ___ 45
Engage in Positive Self-Talk ___ 45
Identify and List Five Positive Things about Yourself Daily ___ 46
Don't Allow Criticism to Break You but Build You Up ___ 46
Embrace your oddity ___ 47
Self-Acceptance Leads to Greater Self-Esteem ___ 47
Practice self-worth inventory ___ 48
HOW LOW SELF-ESTEEM IMPACTS YOUR LIFE ___ 48

Chapter 3: Overcome Stress, Be Comfortable with Yourself and Just Relax _____ 51

What is stress and How Does Stress Affect Your Life? _____ 51
What Are the Benefits of Relieving Stress? _____ 54
Ways to a Stress-Free Life _____ 56
   Don't try to control everything _____ 56
   Spend one hour a day without technology _____ 57
   Take a Time Out _____ 58
   Live in the present moment _____ 59
   Understanding Your Mind _____ 59
Relieve Stress Today and Improve Your Life! _____ 61
Tackle your Problems _____ 63
   Managing Stress at Work _____ 63
   Managing Stress at Home _____ 66
   Managing Financial Stress _____ 67
   Stress and worry _____ 68
How you can use stress to grow _____ 69

Chapter 4: Master Your Emotions and Express Your Feelings Constructively _____ 71

How to change your emotions? _____ 71
Stop Negative Emotions _____ 72
Conditioning Your Mind to Experience More Positive Emotions _____ 75
   You are what you think about most of the time _____ 75
   Thoughts and emotions determine your future _____ 76
Depositing positive thoughts in your mind _____ 76
Changing your emotions by changing your environment _____ 77
How to use your emotions to grow? _____ 78

Chapter 5: Be The Real You and Stop Worrying About What Other People Think 81

Why you have to be real _____ 81

No Matter What, Be Yourself _____ *81*
Learn to Walk Away from Worldly Expectations and Set Your Own Pace _____ *82*
Surround Yourself with Those Who Value Who You are _____ *82*
Don't Take Criticism to Heart _____ *83*
WHAT OTHERS THINK IS IRRELEVANT _____ 84
Remove the Negative from Your Life _____ *84*
Know the Difference Between Constructive Criticism and Harmful Criticism _____ *85*
Not Letting Others' Comments Bother, You _____ *85*
Being Confident in Yourself _____ *86*
Verbally Tell Yourself that You Can Do It and Believing You Can _____ *86*
Go into the Task with Full Energy and Knowing You Will Accomplish it _____ *87*
Don't Allow Negative Thoughts to Change Your Attitude _____ *87*
See it Through Until the End _____ *88*
BUILDING YOUR SELF-WORTH _____ 88
Redefine success _____ *90*
Make your outer appearance a choice and not a yardstick _____ *90*
Seek role models for inspiration, and not comparison _____ *91*
Stop chasing the approval of others _____ *91*
Avoid Negative Talk Completely _____ *92*
Make Celebrating Success a Habit _____ *92*
Validation Comes from Within _____ *93*
STOP WORRYING ABOUT WHAT OTHER PEOPLE THINK __ 93
LET GO & MOVING FORWARD _____ 96

Chapter 6: Build Confidence and Be Assertive Without Having to Fake It _____ 99

WHEN YOU LACK CONFIDENCE, THIS IS WHAT HAPPENS 100

PRACTICAL TIPS TO HELP YOU DEVELOP CONFIDENCE __ 102
   Toss Out Negativity One Day at A Time _____ *102*
   Always Be Prepared _____ *102*
   Everyone Is Better Than You _____ *103*
   Eliminate the Inner Critic _____ *104*
BUILDING SELF-CONFIDENCE _____ 104
   Discover your strengths _____ *105*
   Dare to take risks _____ *105*
   Improve your chances of success _____ *106*
   Track your progress _____ *107*
   Identify your weaknesses _____ *108*
   Plan out your course of action _____ *108*
   Act upon it _____ *109*
   Reward yourself _____ *109*
DRESS WITH CONFIDENCE AND ASSERTIVENESS _____ 110
CARRY YOURSELF WITH THE CONFIDENCE _____ 113
TURN SELF-CONFIDENCE INTO A HABIT _____ 116

Chapter 7: Improve Your Social Skills and Express Yourself _____ 119

SOCIAL SKILLS, WHY IT'S IMPORTANT AND HOW TO GET
   STARTED WITH BUILDING IT _____ 119
   Building Relationships _____ *119*
   More happiness _____ *120*
   Better efficiency and organization _____ *121*
   Enhances confidence and self-worth _____ *121*
   It makes you a good leader _____ *122*
   Increased Confidence _____ *122*
   Increased Personal Safety _____ *122*
   A Better Social Life _____ *123*
DEVELOPING SOCIAL SKILLS _____ 123
   Talk less, listen more _____ *123*
   Avoid Drama Like the Plague _____ *124*
   Think About the Other Person's Mental State ___ *125*
   Take Communication Classes _____ *125*

Read as Often as You Can 126
Consider Your Body Language 126
Acknowledge The Other Person's Feelings 127
Keep Perspectives Realistic and Open 127
Do a Reality Assessment of Your Emotions? 128
Be Mindful of Your Body Language 128
Convey Discomfort Without Raising Hell 129
Learn to change how you think about yourself 129
EFFECTIVE COMMUNICATION PRINCIPLES 130
  Listening 130
  Effectiveness 131
  Perceptual Filters 131
  Patience 132
BREAKING FREE FROM THE LOOP OF NEGATIVE COMMUNICATION PATTERNS 132
LAYING THE FOUNDATION FOR ENHANCED SOCIAL SKILLS 133

Chapter 8: Build Meaningful Relationships by Being Genuine and Without Needing to Fake It 137

GET RID OF TOXIC RELATIONSHIPS 137
  Write a List 138
  Self Affirmations 139
  Connect with Genuine and Positive People 140
  Heal and Stay Hopeful 140
  Keep it Drama Free 141
  Forgive Yourself 141
FACE YOUR FEARS AND INTERACT WITH PEOPLE 142
  Take Baby Steps 142
  Have a Supportive Buddy Around 143
  Think of the Bigger Picture 143
  Take the Plunge 143
MANAGE YOUR SOCIAL LIFE 144
  Upgrade Your Community 146

Choose Who You Surround Yourself With *146*
Be Part of a Community *147*
Invest *147*
Get Support *147*
Productive conflict *148*
Be Inspired *149*
TO BUILD A RELATIONSHIP, THE FOLLOWING PILLARS MUST BE PRESENT. 150
Love *150*
Communication *150*
Commitment *151*
Trust *152*
Honesty *152*
Intimacy *153*
Accept your partner for who he or she really is *153*

Chapter 9: Truly Be Who You Want to Be and Express Yourself Authentically 155

HOW TO BE YOURSELF – EMBRACE YOUR FAULTS 155
DEVELOP YOUR STRENGTHS 157
CELEBRATE YOUR UNIQUENESS 158
WORK ON YOUR BELIEFS 160
FACE YOUR FEAR 162
Face the fear *162*
Evaluate the risk level of the fear *162*
Make an action plan *163*
EXTENDING ACCEPTANCE AND EMPATHY TOWARDS YOURSELF 163
Challenge Your Misleading Thoughts *164*
Accept Yourself *166*
Control Only What's Within Your Reach *166*
Embrace the Idea of Not Being Everyone's Cup of Tea *167*

Chapter 10: Continuously Improve Yourself and Become the Best Person You Can Be 169

RESHAPING YOUR MINDSET _____ 169
MANAGE YOUR TIME, MANAGE YOUR LIFE _____ 170
BUILDING MOTIVATION AND STAY FOCUSED ON YOUR
   GOALS _____ 172
BECOME AWARE OF YOUR THOUGHTS FEELINGS AND
   ACTION _____ 173
FOCUS ON THE SOLUTIONS RATHER THAN THE PROBLEMS 174
LEARN THE LESSONS FAILURE HAS TO OFFER _____ 175
INCREASE FOCUS AND MENTAL CLARITY _____ 176
IMPROVING YOUR APPEARANCE AND PHYSICAL FITNESS 177
OPEN YOURSELF TO MORE OPPORTUNITIES _____ 179
TAKE CARE OF YOUR HEALTH _____ 180
   Taking Better Care of Your Diet_____ 180
   Exercising More Frequently_____ 181
   Receiving Adequate Rest _____ 182
WORK HARDER _____ 183
MAINTAIN SELF-DISCIPLINE _____ 184
KNOW WHAT'S HOLDING YOU BACK? _____ 185
BELIEVE IN YOURSELF & YOUR ABILITIES _____ 186
OVERCOMING LIMITING BELIEFS, SELF-DOUBTS AND
   FEARS _____ 188
ALLOW YOURSELF TO CELEBRATE DAILY WINS _____ 189
KILL THE NEGATIVE SELF-TALK _____ 190
PROGRAM YOURSELF TO BECOME SUCCESSFUL _____ 191
LEARN TO SAY "NO" _____ 192
IDENTIFYING YOUR VALUES & ENFORCING THEM _____ 192
LIVING WITH GRATITUDE _____ 194
RESIST PROCRASTINATION AT ALL COSTS _____ 196
COMMIT YOURSELF TO HAPPINESS _____ 199

Conclusion _____ 201

Introduction

This book contains proven steps and strategies on how to look beyond what others think of you and make your impression on the world in small and tangible ways. Many people lack the self--confidence they need in order to achieve their dreams and goals. What would happen if you could find that confidence and achieve more than you hoped you could? Building confidence is a tough journey, but even the more confident people have suffered with insecurities from time to time.

Even though you may not be able to identify it, many people suffer with self-esteem and confidence issues every day of their lives. In a world that has predetermined expectations for everyone, you want to fit in and show people that you are who you say you are. However, you may not feel like you're doing it right, and that can rob you of your true potential. This book aims to help you find that confidence that you may lack and use it to achieve all of your goals and ambitions.

Self-improvement can have a significant impact on such things as creating better relationships, reducing stress and anxiety, and even improving a person's physical health and wellbeing. Perhaps, most importantly, self-improvement can serve to remove the obstacles that hold an individual back from living the life of their dreams. Subsequently, if there is an area in your life that you wish to transform, exploring the world of self-improvement might just provide the solutions you are looking for.

This book will discuss numerous methods and techniques for improving your life, including many that are practiced by today's most successful people. These techniques will change how you think, speak and even interact with others. They will also help you to create better habits in your day-to-day life—ones that will help eliminate the stress and confusion that can keep you from finding true meaning and contentment in life. By the time you finish reading this book you will not only know the methods and techniques for improving your life, you will also know how to implement them into your day-to-day routine. This will enable you to live a life that takes you closer to your goals each and every day, resulting in you transforming your life into the life of your dreams, filled with the success and happiness you both desire and deserve!

Effective communication forms the basis of both – your personal and professional encounters. The words, actions and gestures you use to connect with people help them understand you and make it easier for you to influence their actions in your favor.

Social skills are all about being a powerful communicator, charismatic leader and persuasive individual. However, the most important yet largely overlooked aspect of social skills is how you make people feel about themselves.

Chapter 1:

Love Yourself and Get Over Self-Hatred And Self-Loathing

Self-Love is a lifelong practice that has to be fully attended to in order to bring about its full effects. In the current era, the law of attraction is very popular and comes with a myriad of benefits. It refers to the fundamental nature of the universe; that we have but one thing in our power, which is our attention. And whatever we turn our attention to, we attract towards us.

Self-hatred: Why don't I love myself

Finding the self is a mystical concept that has been around since ancient times. The 'self' has been described by many names, such as the soul, the over-soul, the atman, the monad, the "I AM" presence, the Christos, the illumined one, and so on. Labels aside, it can be described as who you truly are without any of the social behaviors and attitudes that you have downloaded since birth. It can be 'found' by shedding illusion and peeling away the layers of programming, which can also be called the ego.

The entire process of childhood and socialization is essentially learning how to forget who we really are. Our peers and parents scold us when we do something that does not conform to their viewpoint. As such, we learn how to behave in such a way that we can be accepted. Being part of a group, family or tribe is the single most important social norm. This dates back to a time where non-conformity would have gotten us thrown out of the tribe – likely to starve or freeze to death. Pleasing others is ingrained deep within us, but it is also very harmful in terms of spiritual evolution.

So when born, we experience traumas in forgetting who we are. And we then have to go through the process of forgetting everything we learned in school and through wider society to find our true selves. Sadly, reconnecting is anything but easy in the modern age. Technology ensures that information is everywhere so we will look everywhere but inside – where the self resides.

There is a defined path to find the self "quickly", though the process could still hardly be described as quick. There are more ways to try and find who you really are. It is best likened to the peeling of an onion where only the true self is left. A good place to start is to review all of what has happened to you in this lifetime and the major events. The point is not to wallow in them or take pride in achievements. Just draw a linear map of the major events that happened, what their effect on you was, and try to see the bigger picture. This will help to build a degree of objectivity.

Finding self is an individual process. Nobody has ever self-realized themselves together. It is just not the way that the universe works. There is no way to share creativity or ingenuity because it comes from within. This means that when you are finding the self, the practices that you use and the philosophy that you adopt will be yours alone. If you simply copy what others are doing, then you are already disempowered, and will never find the self. Without making decisions of your own volition, you are not giving yourself any power.

Rediscover Your Real Identity

In the modern world, you may hear that having a high regard for oneself is egotistical, which makes it hard to concentrate on and aspire to love yourself. However, there was once a time earlier on in your life when you were indeed conscious and appreciative of who you really were, and when you were enthusiastic about chasing after things that would facilitate your contentment. This period was during your childhood. Presently, it may be hard to recall and reunite with your inherent self, but try to do just that. Close your eyes, touch your chest, and go back to those days in your early youth, envisioning an occasion in which you were taking part in something that you delighted in and that brought you joy. This is your spirit, the part of you that is aware of your true self and knows how to appreciate it. That person is still alive, but it just may take a little while to rediscover them. During our childhoods, there was rarely any dishonor related to desiring things and making ourselves a priority from time to time. Naturally, as we reach adulthood, we are assigned more accountability for both ourselves and others. Of course, it is rational and obligatory that as we grow older we need to release some of those juvenile temperaments and actions if we are to properly perform as adults are expected to. All the same, it is also true that if we dismiss it entirely, we can also misplace certain mindsets that can in fact add value to our adult lives.

As we endeavor to be accountable and compassionate towards others, we often entirely forget our own desires and happiness, even when people don't return the same well-mannered behaviors that we provide them with. It can even get to the point where after a given point we disregard ourselves completely, regardless of the significance of self-reflection. We end up devoting our entire lives to work and loved ones, especially in the case of having children. Even though it is necessary to provide children with as much care and nurturing as possible, one should always make an effort to create equilibrium between self-care and the care of others who need them. This is actually beneficial to children as well, as they will also be cheerier and mentally healthier if their parents are also happy and satisfied. Therefore, it is important to make sure you have time to fulfill your own needs as well to benefit the entire household. If you ever feel that you have drifted apart from your real, inherent self, call to mind that inner child that was once so content, even if just for a minute. This will assist you in reconnecting with your inner self and get you back on the road to loving yourself. Of course, it could be the case that your childhood wasn't always a joyful time; unfortunately for some people, a happy childhood was something that they imagined but couldn't receive. If this applies to you, it may actually be counterproductive to reflect on this time and draw motivation from it. In this case, it could very well be that a lot of the issues that you identify within yourself were conceived during your childhood. In that regard, you can reflect on that period of your life to determine things that should be amended rather than repeated.

When you resolve to do something, regardless of what it is, it is essential to identify why you wish to accomplish this task and what the end goal is. When aiming to achieve self-love, there are three fundamental questions that you need to consider: why you are doing it, what changes you wish to achieve, and what things you have created for yourself that are standing in your way. With the first question, contemplate what factors in your life have brought you to the decision to work towards loving yourself. There is surely a reason, and you will not be able to achieve your goal until you realize the issue that is motivating you to pursue it. Contemplate your current life, and create a list of three factors that you wish to eliminate or improve upon.

Everyone at some point has formed habitual negative thoughts or actions that keep us from reaching the objectives ahead of us. These things can originate from people we know or from the society that we live in. These roadblocks can prevent you from loving yourself, but it is imperative to keep in mind that once you acknowledge these problems in your way, you can easier push them to the side and overcome them. Coming up with a short list of things that could possibly be standing in your way is significantly more difficult than as with the previous two steps, because this list can seem considerably longer. However, it is important to think of as many as possible, because it is necessary to identify all of them to be able to overcome them. Address each of these problems and think of how they have negatively affected you in the past, and make a deal with yourself that you will not let that cycle repeat itself.

Even though recognizing your problems and resolving to fix them is an important step in the process, there is of course much more to it. As you can probably imagine, changing a problematic situation is not as simple as it may sound. Countless people have trouble making positive changes in their lives, no matter how much they may desire to do so. The fact of the matter is that in the beginning, making life changes can sometimes require compromises and discomfort, which may seem contradictory as you are trying to achieve self-love. It will be necessary to step outside of your box in numerous ways in order to make the changes that you want.

Self-assurance can only be realized when you accept and have faith in yourself, and once you truly achieve that, it cannot be broken and will not require external support. In this respect, even though your initial goal may be to stop substance abuse, this is actually just the first step to achieving self-assurance and confidence, and also improving your physical health. In the end, it all comes down to your center of concentration and what you choose to devote your dynamism to. As soon as you initiate the positive changes and experience the first inkling of their advantages, which will be motivation enough to continue on and never to return to your past destructive ways.

Thoroughly Analyzing How Much You Love Yourself

Try and think of who you really are with disregard to your earlier life, the people in your life, or your present situation. Consider who you are when these elements are removed. If you find this difficult, you must keep trying until you are able to figure it out. If you end up discovering that you have a habit of identifying yourself according to any of those previously mentioned factors, then those are the areas that you need to focus on changing. Then, consider what brings you joy and what factors in your life are significant to you. A characteristic of loving yourself is being able to not only know what your wishes and principles are, but also to indulge in and fulfill them. If you can identify these elements in your life but realize that you have up until this point been postponing or completely neglecting them, this will become an obvious area in which change is needed. Think about how you handle your own feelings; do you directly confront them within yourself, or do you attempt to push them away or mute them? A large factor of self-love is being honest with and aware of yourself. If you can't recognize and admit your emotions, you are not being honest with yourself, and this is something that is necessary in order to move forward.

You can also try and figure out your true self by examining your behaviors. You can find this particularly useful if you notice that you have a habit of doing reckless or thoughtless actions. When you recognize yourself doing these things, think about them and consider how these actions reflect you as a person, including your attitude and state of mind. If you have a slip-up, you can use this guide to recognize what exactly caused you to make an error. Additionally, when working on gathering comprehensive insight of who your true self is and is not, it is vital to make sure that this realization comes from you alone, without the influence of others' opinions. There will inevitably be many people who are accusatory and think that they have a definition of who you are or what you are or are not capable of, and may even think that they know you better than you know yourself; however, this is certainly not true. If you feel that this is not the case, always make sure to never let someone else's thoughts or opinions about you influence how you think or feel about yourself. No one knows you better than you do, and keeping this in mind is one of the most important things that will progress you towards loving yourself.

Learning to Love Yourself

You will be put on the right track and guided through the process of getting into the right mindset, much increasing your chances of success. Whatever change you go through in your life, there are four main phases: realization, contemplation, changing, and assimilation The first phase is realization, because you cannot expect to achieve results if you do not know what it is that needs to be improved upon.

Many people who are unhappy with life are unhappy with themselves. They don't think that they measure up to the people around them, or what is expected of them. This is, of course, nonsense but a depressed person won't believe that. In order to overcome issues that you face with your personal self-esteem, sit in front of a mirror and look at yourself.

Observation

The point of the exercise is to show you that no one actually measures up to every standard and that some people who were born at a disadvantage can actually be proud and confident because they are happy inside. When you learn to be comfortable in the skin you're in, you begin to gain confidence and your self-esteem gets much better. You see yourself as a whole person and are able to move through life without letting other people's criticism touch you. It really is as simple as that.

The Mirror Exercise

You are probably your worst enemy right now. Most people who are depressed and anxious find that the unhappiness comes from inside. Thus, look at yourself in the mirror. Are you the kind of person you would want as a friend? When you are depressed and it shows on the outside, the inside is going to automatically feel worse. Thus, you need to take action. Wash your face, clean your teeth, brush your hair and dress in reasonable clothes. Stop neglecting yourself because it doesn't help your cause at all. When you feel dowdy and you don't bother with yourself, you make yourself feel even worse. This is something you can do something about and you need to because you can't feel very good about yourself when all you do is neglect yourself. It's not about looks. It's about self-respect and when you start to build that up, then confidence is something that happens as a result. Of course, you can have a makeover of your hairstyle or do more to make yourself look great, but the first steps are yours and yours alone.

Get into a routine again because that routine serves a purpose. It gives you times to groom yourself, to eat properly, to sleep for the right amount of time and to get you out of the funk of depression being demonstrated in your life.

Being Present

One of the usual responses to the question, "How would you make a child feel loved?" is, "I'd give that child undivided attention." We are usually so caught up in the "busyness" of our lives that we rarely focus on the needs of our inner child. So often we put all the shoulds, have-tos and responsibilities in our life first. When we do manage to spend time with the child (whether our inner child or an external one), often our minds are off in some distant place, thinking about a past event or worrying about the future. Consequently, even though we are physically there, the child does not feel our presence. One significant way to love your inner child is to be present, even if it is only for a few minutes each day. Just as focusing attention on a child even for a short time can have a powerful and lasting effect, so can a similar focus nourish your inner child. Whether meditating, gazing at a beautiful nature scene, or just noticing the feelings in your emotional or physical body, spending a short period of time being fully present each day can do wonders.

Spending Fun Time

Another point people mention regarding loving a child is making time to do something the child finds enjoyable—a practice that also nurtures your inner child. This means setting aside time to do whatever would please your inner child, letting it know that it is a priority and that you are serious about establishing a new relationship. As you practice this you will begin to experience definite changes in your inner child's behavior and attitude. I know that for me taking time to do enjoyable things has had a particularly strong, direct effect on my life.

It is important when scheduling an activity for your inner child, that it doesn't have a particular goal, just that it be something fun and enjoyable. Do what you love to do for its own sake, not for the benefit you are going to derive from it later. You do not have to be good at this activity. Often as children we enjoyed certain activities but weren't as good at them as some prescribed ideal, so we stopped doing them. The important thing is that the activity feels good to you and that you can lose yourself in it. Ask yourself what activity might you begin or get back to. Does a smile come to your face when you think about being in nature, playing sports, or doing something adventurous like skydiving or rock climbing? Or does doing something quieter like reading or playing chess bring you joy? Does dancing, singing, or painting sound like fun? Even if you have never done it before, it is never too late to start.

Spending time with your inner child in any one of these playful, creative, or nurturing ways may require rearranging your priorities. If having a more loving relationship with your inner child and all the joy, aliveness, and creativity that it can potentially bring is a high priority for you then you will be willing to pay the price of eliminating or rearranging activities necessary to achieve this.

Communicate

It is also important to be aware of how we speak. Without realizing it, we often communicate to ourselves in derogatory phrases we learned from our family or society, using put-downs and tones of voice that inhibit the inner child. A powerful exercise for communicating with your inner child is to regularly write her or him. Start off with something like, "What is going on for you?" or "What are you feeling about?" or just "What are you feeling?" Then let the words flow. You can respond, engaging in a dialogue, or just let the child speak freely. You will often be amazed at what comes out.

Clear Your Mind of Destructive Feelings

As you advance on your path to loving yourself, you will surely experience some setbacks and discouragement throughout the process. You may regress into your earlier mindset that it isn't appropriate to be focusing on yourself so much, or that you should be concentrating on making others happy and comfortable over yourself. Something that can greatly assist in clearing these thoughts from your mind is to not only clear your mind, but literally cleanse yourself, by treating yourself to a nice bath or shower. You may wonder how this could possibly assist you in learning how to love yourself, but if you think about a bath or shower as a symbolic cleansing of your mind, it can really ease your mind and fortify your deletion of negative thoughts. While you're physically washing your body, think of all of the debris in your mind being rinsed away as well. Your body feels clean and refreshed, and so does your mind.

Consider Why You Think Self-Love is Important

Thinking about why you value self-love is imagining the difference that it could make it your own life. Think about how different things would be if you appreciated and were happy with yourself. Concentrate on the benefits of valuing and reveling in yourself as a person, as well as your capabilities and enjoyments. Don't just reflect on this as a passing thought, but really take some time and deeply consider why you consider self-love so important and the positive changes it could make in your life. If need be, go to a quiet place and close your eyes to focus better. If you do this regularly, those notions of egocentrism and disdain will continue to fade away. You will also be able to keep your objectives in sight and what advantages loving yourself can provide you with. Keeping this in mind will help you further on your path to achieving your goals of self-appreciation and love.

Realizing the significance of loving yourself and considering how it can positively change your life are both necessary, but it is equally as important to be aware of false connotations associated with loving yourself. For starters, self-love is not defined as disdain or selfishness. We don't want to appear egotistical or that we value ourselves above others or think that we deserve more than anyone else, but loving yourself does not mean that this is how you feel. Loving and appreciating your inherent self is completely different than viewing yourself as of a higher status than others. If you really love yourself, there is no need for competition or authority. As a matter of fact, if you genuinely achieve self-love, you can appreciate and acknowledge your abilities and consider how they can help other people in your life, and help you to become the best version of yourself. A vain person does not consider these things, and truly only thinks about themselves and their priority over other people, not caring how it will affect those around them. Loving yourself also is not by any means defined as physical pleasure. Lastly, loving yourself is absolutely not aimed to impress or gain the approval of anyone else in the world except for yourself. The point of loving yourself is that it concentrates on your own welfare, contentment, and requirements.

The Importance of Radical Self-Love

Radical self-love refers to loving yourself no matter what is happening in the world, and no matter what you have done (whether positive or negative). It is very easy to judge yourself, compare yourself to others, and even be cruel to yourself in the world that we live in. In order to be healthy, it is important to love yourself no matter what the circumstances. We cannot depend on the love of others to boost us up. We all want somebody to love and care for us, to boost our self-esteem, however, your own self-love cannot be defined by the love that others give you. In order to truly be loved, you must first understand that self-love is the most important factor.

Chapter 2:

Overcome Social Anxiety, Shyness, Self-Consciousness and Build Self-Esteem

Overcoming Shyness and social anxiety

Being shy is one of the most difficult hurdles to overcome mentally as you work towards building your self-esteem. But that is exactly why you're here and reading this book because you want to improve yourself and become a better, more confident, effective version of yourself. To be the person you have always wanted to become, and the first step towards that is to work on overcoming your shyness if this is something you have been struggling with.

What you need to remember is that no matter how impossible a challenge may seem, there is always a way to overcome it. To start living your best life as the new and improved you, it starts with first acknowledging that there is a problem that needs to be fixed. Depending on the severity of your shyness, it may or may not be impacting your life more than you would like.

Start by Accepting and Acknowledging Your Fears

This may be the last thing in the world that you feel like doing, but it is a necessary part of the process. Running away or living in denial is never the way to get to the root of the problem, and no matter what your fear may be. The best thing you can do for yourself is to accept and acknowledge it.

Changing Your Thought Patterns

One of the main causes for shyness and a lack of confidence in social situations is often because we put too much pressure on ourselves and have unrealistic expectations, sometimes even before the situation has happened. You may worry about not being able to live up to expectations, worry about what happens if you say the wrong thing and risk making a fool of yourself, or maybe even worry that nobody will like you or what you have to say.

Changing Your Focus

Focus on who is present around you and what each person does. Concentrate on the things that they are saying so you will be able to respond and reciprocate appropriately. Be present in the conversation so that your mind has no time to drift and worry about being shy.

Love the Sound of Your Voice

Start getting used to loving the sound of your own voice, you're going to need to if you want to be comfortable in social situations. Record yourself having pretend conversations and then playback those recordings to see how you sound. Do you like what you hear? Are you speaking clearly? Are you mumbling too much, or articulating your words well? Does the conversation flow smoothly? Pretending to have conversations with yourself may feel silly, but by listening to your own recording will help you notice patterns and the inflection of your voice.

Build a more practical and reasonable image of others

Everyone is fighting their limitations and challenges, and no one is perfect. Have a realistic view of others. They are humans with a set of strengths and weaknesses, and they falter too. They also make mistakes or go wrong in their judgment. It is highly unrealistic to believe everyone is superior to you or better than you.

Tackle your inhibitions and fears

Avoiding these fears lead to even greater discomfort and phobia, which magnifies the issue. The more we try to escape from something rather than tackling it, the more our condition snowballs into bigger issues. Facing your challenges is the first step towards eliminating them. For example, if a specific social scenario such as public speaking makes you anxious or break out into uncontrollable sweat, rather than fearing it, start facing it. Tell yourself what you stand to lose by not overcoming your fear of public speaking. You will be unable to share your ideas and inputs with others, while also hampering the development of business associations.

Have more faith in people

Rather than believing that people are always evaluating your negatively, approach them from the point of trust. Understand that people's intentions are not questionable all the time.

You may have had instances in the past where people betrayed your trust. However, attempt to move on from the past by developing greater forgiveness and tolerance. Understand that a few encounters with bad people don't make the world or everyone bad. There are positive and negative people, just like there are sweet and rotten apples.

Take risks to move outside your comfort zone

Take small steps to meet and interact with people who share similar interests and passions. Train your mind to watch out for clues when people want to connect with you. Challenge your thoughts each time they attempt to prevent you from doing something. Each time you find yourself fearing something, start doing it in a small way. You don't have to go and grab the stage directly. Start by opening up to a few people or addressing a small group.

Build your patience, courage, will-power, perseverance

Each day take a tiny step towards accomplishing your goal of being a more confident and socially relaxed person with courage and patience. Take note of the smallest successes so you can continue the momentum with bigger success stories. Be aware of the fact that just because you suffer from shyness or social anxiety doesn't mean you have to be condemned to a life of loneliness, misery, and isolation.

Build a more reasonable, practical and balanced picture of yourself

Start believing yourself by developing a more realistic image. You aren't really inferior to all the people, all the time. You are not unworthy of being loved by other people. Have greater confidence in your abilities and potential. Each time you find yourself undermining your own potential or qualities, think about instances when you did something really well. Don't believe things will go wrong all the time before even getting to the situation. Each time you find yourself indulging in self-criticism, beat it with evidence that proves the contrary.

Manage your breath to regulate emotional reactions

Practice breathing and controlling your breath. When you are anxious, you are often short of breath or breathe quickly/rapidly. A quickened pace of breath makes the psychological condition even worse. It may cause anxiety, hot flashes, sweating, and dizziness.

Therefore, you eliminate this shyness or physiological, social anxiety symptoms by learning to control your breath. Start by sitting in a peaceful place that is free from distractions. Sit in a comfortable and relaxed posture on a chair or the floor. Focus on your breath. Start counting slowly as you inhale deeply, following by counting while you exhale deeply.

Avoid negative thoughts

Getting rid of these ideas is critical to the process of recovery. If you want to live a social anxiety-free life, start working towards replacing these self-limiting thoughts with more positive ones. You can either enlist professional help or try to eliminate these thoughts on your own. Identify when and how these automatic negative thoughts make their way inside your mind.

Shyness or social anxiety originates from a deep-rooted need to imagine the worst. You always imagine people don't like you or think you are stupid or perceive you in a highly negative manner. The realistic truth is often far from it.

Make daily reflection a habit

You hold limitless potential within you that simply needs to be unlocked! Take time out to reflect upon who you are and what you are capable of accomplishing. It will help restore a sense of balance and coherence in your life. Establish a higher sense of purpose and peace that will make your life more meaningful.

Set aside a few hours of your day for self-reflection. Ask yourself questions such as, what is my true potential? What are my positive traits, skills, and strengths? How can I contribute to make other people's lives more meaningful? What am I capable of accomplishing that I haven't yet accomplished?

Identify problems and fears, along with their triggers

By focusing on your problems, you are able to identify triggers that are furthering harming your condition. It gives you the opportunity to focus on a solution – to surround yourself with more positive and inspiring people in your life who lift you instead of breaking you apart. If something or someone is augmenting your fear of being judged negatively by others, look for ways to avoid the person or situation. By identifying things that make matters worse, you can focus on solutions.

Building Self-Esteem

Self-esteem can be defined as the image a person has of himself. It is a very important factor in determining the kinds of experiences an individual will have in life and his emotional reactions to them. He or she is the one who is actually the source of his own anguish by choosing to listen to his inner critic and wallowing in depressive and negative emotional states. To get out of this vicious cycle of self-abuse, there are various means to help a person build his self-worth.

Control your emotions

A person should thus learn to suspend judgment in any particular situation and think carefully before acting.

Furthermore, empathy is another component of emotional intelligence. A person needs to understand the emotional setup of different people and treat those people according to their emotional reactions. In doing so, an individual can easily read another person's emotional state and avoid being emotionally engaged in the situation.

People who are emotionally intelligent have a better attitude and outlook on life. They perform well at their jobs and respond better to challenging situations.

Conquering Your Inner Critic

Everyone has an inner critic. This is the voice that tells you that the job you did might not have been so great after all, and that you don't look very good or shouldn't feel good about yourself. Some let the voice get too strong, and this can quickly wreck your self-esteem. It is normal to have some spells that are worse than others, but when your critic becomes the predominant voice in your head then it's time to learn how to conquer it.

The first step is realizing what your points of insecurity are. Journaling can help you pinpoint these aspects, as can gauging your mood at certain points during the day using useful scales such as the Rosenberg Self-Esteem Scale. Checking your self-esteem before a project and then again after can help you see if your work is bringing you down, or maybe your self-esteem grows after completing a household chore. Recognizing these patterns is a very important first step to owning and controlling your inner critic.

Practice, Practice, Practice

When looking to change your life and become the person you want to be, there is nothing like practice. Many people associate practice with just sports or education, but practice applies to every aspect of life and can be invaluable in becoming who you want to be. Nobody can change overnight and practice can be applied to every aspect of life to help you become the best version of yourself.

Practice doesn't have to be a person just repeating the same action over and over again; it can happen on paper or while playing out scenarios in your head. Lists and realizing what path one needs to follow are good ways to induce practice in your head, and think ahead to what you'll do during when confronted with a particular situation. Living through situations before they happen can be great social practice and will help you think on your feet so that you don't freeze in critical life situations.

Using Affirmations to Change Your Thinking

Positive affirmations are positive words and thoughts that program your mind, similar to the way a computer is programmed. They help you focus on your goals or desires. Affirmations create mental pictures in your conscious mind. The mental pictures in your conscious mind then affect the way your subconscious mind works.

Changing Your Personal Narrative

Your personal narrative is crucial to how you interpret your reality because, believe it or not, all the things that we take as objective truth are actually judgments. That is all they are. Two people can look at the same set of facts and walk away two totally different interpretations. Their personal narratives determine the difference in these interpretations. When you work on building up on your self-confidence through working on your self-esteem, you necessarily have to swap out your personal narrative. There has to be certain changes in your personal narrative for this inside-out process to work.

Change Your Mental Patterns

The funny thing about people's perception of reality is that, in many cases, their perception of reality is really just a product of their mental habits. If you habitually interpret things, in the worst way possible, it is very easy for you to conclude that this is the only way people can interpret these signals. This is the only judgment they can have. After all, since you automatically conclude things are a certain way when you get particular feedback or specific stimuli, then that must be reality. Well, it may turn out that you think that way accordingly because it is your mental habit. Your mental patterns are set up in such a way that you always end up with a certain conclusion.

Once Your Self-Esteem is Positive, You Project It Out

After you have gone through the process of changing your self-perception, swapping out or modifying your personal narrative, and identifying, disrupting and replacing your mental patterns, the next step is to project it out. In other words, you go from the internal to the external. You go from emotions to intentions to actions.

Create an ideal self-image

Perhaps the most common form of creating an ideal self-image is to find a role model. This can take the form of a fictional character, such as someone in a book or a movie, or it can take the form of a real person. In the case of a fictional character there is the danger of trying to achieve an ideal that is somewhat unrealistic. After all, that is one of the benefits of fiction—it doesn't have to conform to the rules of the real world. However, there can be a great many benefits to aspiring to a fictional role model.

Reflect on your past

Interestingly enough, another way to build self-esteem is to take the time to reflect on your past. Most people who lack self-esteem usually want to escape their past. They are either ashamed of certain events in their life or they are simply unsatisfied with how their life has taken shape. However, the truth of the matter is that you are always your worst critic. This means that you hold yourself to the highest standards while also finding the greatest amount of fault in everything you do. While such high self-expectation can be healthy to a point it can also prevent you from taking the positives from your life experiences. No matter how disappointing your past may seem, the fact is that there will be plenty of things to take satisfaction in. By taking the time to reflect on your past you can begin to see the positives that may have eluded you before, thereby gaining a more favorable view of yourself and the qualities you possess.

Provide support for others

When you provide support, even just emotional or moral support, you become vital to someone else's success. Needless to say, it is impossible to feel worthless when someone becomes dependent on the support you provide. This can boost a person's sense of self-esteem more than just about any other method discussed, here or elsewhere. Therefore, if you want to feel better about yourself take the time to make a difference in someone else's life. You can choose to volunteer at a charity or soup kitchen, you can engage in a mentoring program, or you might simply offer encouragement and support to those around you whenever you find them struggling. Even the smallest token of support can go a long way to changing another person's life, and thus, improving your sense of self-worth.

Finding Self-Esteem When You Feel at Odds with Yourself

Engage in Positive Self-Talk

It might be crazy at first, but take some time to engage yourself in positive self-talk. I recommend that you stand in front of the mirror so that you can look yourself in the eyes. Tell yourself that you are capable and able to do whatever you set your mind to. No matter what struggles you face, if you go into each day with a positive and willing attitude, you will be able to get more done than if you just float through your day.

Identify and List Five Positive Things about Yourself Daily

Struggling with low self-esteem makes it so that you view yourself in a negative light most of the time. It is nearly impossible to be confident if you don't feel positive about yourself. So, take some time and find your positives. This might be difficult to do at first, but sit down on a daily basis and list five positive things about yourself and your life. Once you begin to see the positive side to yourself and your life, you will begin to feel a boost in your self-esteem and confidence. If this doesn't work immediately, don't give up. It might take some time to break through the negativity that you have around you!

Don't Allow Criticism to Break You but Build You Up

When suffering with low self-esteem, every bit of criticism cuts you deep down. It can be difficult to ignore some of the criticism that comes your way.

Embrace your oddity

Everyone's odd. Get that through your thick skull. Seriously. No joke. Real story. People might play a good game hiding this fact, but it's not going to go away. Everybody's odd. Yeah, that's right. I'm not talking about stuff that you do that makes you feel guilty. Like if you have this "unusual habit" of killing homeless people on the weekends, that's not what I'm talking about.

Self-Acceptance Leads to Greater Self-Esteem

Now that you have embraced your oddity, congratulations. You are definitely several steps away to fully accepting yourself. Self-acceptance is crucial to a healthy self-esteem. You will never find yourself worthy, capable or good enough if you don't accept yourself. Learn to fully accept.

You have to incorporate it so much that it changes how you feel about things. It has to have some sort of emotional effect. This is how you learn to accept yourself fully. This is how you learn to love different parts of yourself. You have to remember that most people love certain parts of themselves but hate everything else.

Practice self-worth inventory

Give yourself enough time to compile a massive self-worth inventory. This is your time. This is a celebration of everything and anything great about you. Anything that's noteworthy and positive, list it down. Knock yourself out.

How Low Self-Esteem Impacts Your Life

Because it has the capacity to keep you from doing many things, having a low self-esteem can reduce the quality of the life you're living. You may find yourself avoiding places, things, and people that you love because you are afraid of what might happen. You fear that you will not be able to stand up or account for yourself. You may also begin to experience depression and anxiety, sometimes with tragic results, because you do not know how to handle or manage things as a result of your low self-esteem.

When you are caught in a place of low self-esteem, you may also find yourself holding onto grudges. This means that you stay in victim-mode for an extended period of time, blaming others for why you feel the way you do and struggling to forgive and move forward. You may even feel like the past is continually haunting you and you cannot seem to escape from it. These are all common side effects of having a low sense of self-esteem.

Through the course of our lives, our self-esteem can be affected by many things. Some people may experience low self-esteem as a result of their childhood, or it may develop later in adulthood as a result of abuse, excessive ongoing stress, or traumatic events. On the other hand, people may experience positive or healthy self--esteem because they have been adequately supported and encouraged throughout childhood and have gone on to experience equally healthy interactions in adulthood.

The common factors known to create low self-esteem are linked to early childhood. Those who were raised in abusive or dysfunctional homes in their formative years can have symptoms that reflect a negative impact on their self-esteem. They may find themselves feeling incapable of living up to someone's standards or regularly trying to fade into the background to avoid dysfunction and abuse. Generally, their idea of what normal interactions look like mirrors unhealthy ones, giving them a false perception of the world around them.

If low self-esteem is developed later in adulthood and was not present in childhood, it may be as a result of ongoing stress or traumatic events. For example, relationship breakdowns, struggles with family or career, incidents of bullying by coworkers or friends, financial burdens, and other such experiences common in adulthood can all contribute to reduced self-esteem. While these individuals will likely have an easier time regaining a healthy self-esteem due to having understood what possessing it felt like, it will still take time and practice to return to that point.

Individuals who have a healthy self-esteem in adulthood are believed to have been raised in a home that supports and encourages individuals, promoting their independence while also providing adequate support to achieve it. They are generally given many coping tools during their upbringing that allow them to feel confident about tackling life's adversities. As a result, these individuals will go on to experience happier and healthier adult lives.

Chapter 3:

Overcome Stress, Be Comfortable with Yourself and Just Relax

What is stress and How Does Stress Affect Your Life?

In general, stress refers to your body's response to any situation that demands change. It can be a result of either positive or negative experiences.

However, most of us tend to associate stress with physical, mental, or emotional tension, anxiety, and worries. Problems encountered in life usually trigger it. It can include problems at work, strain in interpersonal relationships, or uncertainties about the future. It can be trivial, like your car breaking down, or life-changing, like learning that you have been laid off from your job.

This is a difficult question to answer because chronic stress affects you in so many ways that we won't be able to cover all of them in this book. However, the effects of stress on your life are still very negative. In fact, stress might affect you negatively in every way you can possibly think of. This can really seem scary, but you should take it as a reminder that relieving stress is one of the most important things you can do to make your life better.

When you ask people which symptoms they experience in association with stress, these are some of the most common answers:

- Headache
- Fatigue
- Muscle tension
- Upset stomach
- Teeth grinding
- Urge to cry
- Anxiety
- Low energy
- Anger or irritability
- Dizziness
- Low sex drive
- Depression
- Insomnia
- Tingling in extremities
- Change in appetite
- Lethargy
- Rapid pulse

- Restlessness

These symptoms are common side effects and signs of too much stress, and they can be very unpleasant. They are also difficult to get rid of if you don't use the right methods. Unfortunately, many people use stress-relieving methods that only further aggravate their chronic stress, rather than actually relieve it.

Many people also experience symptoms and side effects that they might not know are connected to chronic stress. This is because chronic stress changes your body in a negative way, which can create severe health issues and have many side effects. In other words, stress doesn't just give you unpleasant symptoms that you can feel right away. It also destroys your body, which can create much more severe symptoms and is often at the root cause of chronic diseases. In fact, stress can be, and often is, a contributing factor to almost every chronic disease known to mankind. It is also often at the root cause of relationship issues and many other things that you really want to avoid in your life.

However, I don't want you to be too stressed about having to relieve stress, because that will only cause more stress. So, trust that the methods in this book will help you lower your stress levels in an easy and relaxed way that will make your life better and also make *you* healthier.

What Are the Benefits of Relieving Stress?

Now you know that stress is something that you really want to minimize. You might be a little scared and slightly depressed after going through the horrible effects of stress, but I'm pleased to tell you that all that is going to change in this chapter. Because all the adverse side effects that you might experience from chronic stress mean that you will also receive many benefits from relieving stress.

These are some of the fantastic benefits you are likely to experience when you start relieving stress:
- Less anxiety
- Depression relief
- Better mood
- Increased happiness
- Weight loss
- Better relationships
- Better health
- Fewer infections
- Better social life
- Improved ability to relax and reduce stress immediately
- More energy
- Better functioning of the entire body (including liver, gut, heart, brain, adrenals, and mitochondria)

- Become a calmer and more relaxed person
- Be a healthier person overall
- Perform better in all aspects of life
- Better physical performance
- Better mental performance
- Improved memory
- Less irritability
- Fewer food cravings
- Better hormonal balance
- Prevent and heal chronic diseases
- Improved mindset and higher self-esteem
- Better sleep (which will also help with everything else)

What you should also be able to see from all these benefits is that relieving stress starts a positive cycle. Once you start relieving stress, your mood will improve, your memory and mental performance will become better, your sleep will be better, you will have more energy, you will be healthier, and the list just keeps going on and on. All sorts of positive benefits will continue to show up, and they will create new benefits and a better quality of life. This will keep improving your life and make you a better, happier, smarter, faster, and healthier human being overall.

Ways to a Stress-Free Life

Stress takes on different forms. It can be mild, which is something that you can easily overcome, or it could be something more severe, something that can exhaust you of your energy and resources.

When you feel that you can no longer perform well in your job, or when you can no longer think straight, or when you think that you are not anymore getting the results that you want to achieve, you are likely undergoing severe stress. At this point, it is not advisable to continue with what you are doing. Just like a machine that has been excessively used, people inefficiently function when they are under severe stress. Eliminating the stressors is not easy but there are ways you can do it.

Don't try to control everything

People have the tendency to control everything: their time, money, and other people. What they don't know is that they get most of the stress comes from trying to control everything. It's not bad to be carefree every once in a while. Give yourself some freedom by not thinking about your bills at home, your work deadlines and the traffic jam outside. Recognize that at the moment these things are out of your control.

You can avoid thinking about them. Change your mindset. You can use the analogy of a dresser. In the bottom drawer you can store all your stresses and worries. In the top drawer you can store all your happy thoughts and things you're grateful for. So if you're having difficulty changing your mindset or thoughts, go ahead and place them in the bottom drawer and grab something from the top one.

Spend one hour a day without technology

It is true that technology plays an important role in people's lives. However, it is also true that it takes up a large part of one's time. People are meant for interaction and socialization. Though technology, like smartphones, tablets and computers are meant for communication, people nowadays forget and do not seem to bother talking with their classmates, co-workers and neighbors. It is as if their minds have been taken over by these gadgets.

These gadgets can be a source of additional stress. Spending one hour a day (or longer) without them would be a helpful way of relieving your stress. It can be very challenging for some to not check their email or look at their phone for even one hour. Instead of interacting with your smartphone or computer, talk with the people around you, laugh out loud with them and share stories with them. You'll see how refreshing and energizing this can be.

Take a Time Out

Time out is for those who are brave enough to take a step back and rethink of everything. Taking a timeout does not mean giving up; it just means that there are some things that you need to take care of before proceeding to the next step. In a sense, it's a way to unwind and look at the big picture and refocus on what is important about whatever you are currently working on.

Stress often results from too much work and not giving your body or mind enough time to relax. Give yourself a break from working. Taking short work breaks each hour increases productivity. Even a short 2-5-minute break to stretch your body, or 5 minutes to walk around or 5 minutes to step outside and get some fresh air will help. When you continue working despite exhaustion, you may produce unsatisfactory results that can further aggravate your stress. Some people like to meditate and others like to take a walk to clear their mind. So go ahead and take that timeout.

Live in the present moment

Most of the anxiety, worry, and stress that you feel arise from thinking about the future or the past. You stress about 'what if's'. What if you did this or what if you did not do that? You worry whether it's going to rain or whether you can meet the deadline of your assignment. Live in the present so that much of your worries and anxiety will be eliminated.

Understanding Your Mind

Our minds sometimes find it difficult to discern between reality and thought. Now that we are going to have a closer relationship with our mind and body, we need to understand a little more about it. First things first. Your body is your best friend.

It has been patiently waiting for this day. However, you will quickly see that your body can sometimes fail to differentiate between perception and reality. If I ask you to imagine holding a lemon in your hand you can quickly get a sense of that. You know what a lemon looks and feels like, and you know how it smells even before it has been cut. You can imagine moving it around in your hand and sniffing it, feeling the skin. Is it slightly pitted or smooth, and how fresh does it smell?

Now, in your imagination take a big bite into that lemon, and another bite, and then try, if you can, to cram most of it into your mouth. It will depend on how big your lemon is of course. What is happening to your taste buds in your mouth and your general reactions? Do you get a sense of almost reeling from the onslaught of lemon flooding your mouth: your saliva flowing freely, and a sense of a 'screwed up' face from what it would be like to cram that much fresh juicy lemon into your mouth?

Ok, that was just an experiment to show you how your body believes totally what you tell it. Take a refreshing normalizing breath, breathe fully in, hold it for a few moments, then sigh as you breathe out. You can thank your body and tell it that the lemon is all gone, and everything is fine!

The same thing is happening all day long when your unconscious thoughts are racing through your mind at sixty to the dozen, perceiving all sorts of situations; even worrying about things in the future that have not yet happened, and possibly never will. Or maybe you are harping back on the past and beating yourself up about something you did or said; or maybe something you could have said or done if you had thought in time.

Get real – it's done and gone! The only thing you have any real control over is the 'now', and even that 'now' has just gone into the past! Your life is happening, right now, in front of you, so you need to wise up and get back into the present moment. That is why the present is called that—it is a gift, the gift of now.

Once we understand this fact we can use it very effectively to help create the life of our dreams. Now we know our brains only know what we tell them, and not necessarily the **actual facts**, we can understand where positive affirmations come into it. However, we do have to be aware of other factors. We have a safety cadet that is constantly on watch, looking and listening for anything that looks or sounds suspect. Remember that owl? If you make a statement that is out of line with your real understanding or what your body can currently relate to, it is going to flag it up.

Relieve Stress Today and Improve Your Life!

You should be proud of yourself. At least, I'm proud of you. And I'm happy for you. You have now done something very important. Something that few people do. You have taken action towards controlling your stress levels, and you have taken a huge step towards improving your life.

However, this is also a necessary step. We live in a world packed with stressors everywhere we go. We spend too much time in front of screens, on social media, phones, and tablets. We're constantly active. Many of us are almost always in **fight-or-flight mode**. Instead, we spend too much time in environments with bad air quality and bad lightning, and we're constantly overexposed to toxins from food, water, air, personal care products, and other sources. **Even worse than that, most of us don't have a good social life.** We spend too little time with the people we love and too much time alone or with people we don't really like. There are so many stressors in modern society, and it's easy to let them destroy your life.

However, I trust that you won't let that happen to yourself. You know that it's more important than ever to have daily habits that can instantly lower your stress levels and give you more energy. You know it's important to have a good, supportive community around you. You know that good sleep is incredibly important. You know that you can make your body resilient to stress, so you are much better able to handle stressful situations. Basically, you know how to be in charge of your own stress levels. And, when you control your own stress levels, you become happier, and your life becomes better.

I genuinely hope that you will use all of this powerful knowledge that you have gained in this book to lower your stress levels and improve your life. You truly deserve a better life with less stress.

However, I know that it can very difficult to do the right thing for yourself, especially when you're stressed. I know it can be difficult to start and to keep a daily meditation practice. I know it can be difficult to get high-quality sleep every night.

Tackle your Problems

The first step to stress management is to really find out what's bothering you the most in your life. Whether it is your job that is stressing you out, or your family life, or your financial situation, or a sense of dissatisfaction buried deep-down inside of you that doesn't let you rest and relax. You, as a person, need to prioritize your life and then begin to manage your stress by tackling that aspect of your life that's bothering you the most.

Let's say it's your hostile workplace, a disgruntled boss and a dead-end job that is the most stressful in your life.

Managing Stress at Work

Do you feel like you are stuck in a dead-end job that you are starting to loath? Are you reluctant to come to get out of your bed in the morning everyday because you can't bear the thought of coming to office? Then you are definitely not alone!

A lot of people feel dissatisfied and discontented at their jobs and are thus stressed at the thought of continuing but only do because of the financial security or the stature that the job provides. However, this is truly not the way to carry on, because when you are not happy with your job, you cannot give your 100% concentration or your full devotion to it.

If you really are unhappy with your situation at the office, then perhaps it is time for you to look elsewhere. Was there a job offer somewhere else that maybe paid a little less but was something you could enjoy doing? Did you always want to work in marketing but are stuck at a law firm because the designation is more prestigious?

We believe that it is time for you to go for your dreams and do something that you really feel like doing. When you find yourself in the right job, at the right company, your stress level will automatically disappear and you will be free to live your life in a much happy manner.

Another problem that people face in the workplace is not being appreciated in their work. They feel like they are being walked over by their other colleagues who are taking up the credit for their efforts while they are left in the background feeling unappreciated and invisible.

This problem is also very common in the workplace and the only way to get out of this is to be more assertive at work. Being assertive means to be able to stand up for one's rights and be bold and clear about your needs to be valued and respected for what you have done. If you are not vocal about what you expect from your job, no one else will.

Some people really have a hard time saying 'no' to others, just get bombarded with additional work that is not their own, or responsibilities that are not theirs. Thus, having to bear the added stress from added work. For them also, it is very important to be assertive at the workplace and know where to draw the line between helping others and when to stop being a doormat to other's needs.

You have to learn to say 'no' unless you want to stay stressed doing other people's work for them and hating yourself while you are doing it.

Financial dissatisfaction at work, i.e., not earning enough, is another important cause of stress at the workplace. Many people feel that they are not earning enough at work compared to the amount of effort and time that they are putting on.

Many people have a tendency to take on more responsibility on themselves than what is healthy. They do not trust others to do the job as perfectly as they can. These people are usually perfectionists who are always adding on extra stress into their lives. The best advice for these type of people is to let go of some of the works that others can possibly do better than them. No one needs to do everything in an office themselves; it's not healthy or possible, and it would certainly not be efficient.

Letting go of some of the responsibilities is an extremely efficient way of relieving oneself of extra stress in the workplace.

Although more in the workplace, strain and anxiety is also found at home and within our near and dear ones.

Managing Stress at Home

The most common problem is perhaps the increasing distance between couples and the dissatisfaction in relationships.

Every relationship has its ups and downs. While it is not healthy to stick with each other every waking moment, it is actually important to set aside some time to spend with family and loved ones. Communication between couples is extremely important, so if you have a hunch that your spouse of your partner is aggrieved with you, it is the best advice to quietly sit down with each other and talk things through. You will be surprised to see how easily solutions to every problem can come out when you are willing to communicate honestly.

If you are stressed because you feel like you are stuck in a relationship that is neither moving forward nor backwards, then again, you are not alone. Many people feel somewhat stuck when they are in a relationship that is possibly not the best option for them. Whether it is a marriage that is not working out or a relationship, you have to face the facts that something is missing from your chemistry.

Couple's counseling or marriage counseling is an excellent way to resolve unspoken conflicts in a relationship. If counseling does not work, perhaps the best option is to sever the relationship than live in stress for years to come.

Financial stress is also a very important factor to consider.

Managing Financial Stress

In this commercial age, almost all of us are guilty of spending more than what we are earning, thanks to credit cards. Many of us are in debt and overdrawn from the bank. This is a reason for stress for millions of people all over the world who are desperately looking for ways to pay back their bank before they are bankrupted.

For people who are dangerously overdrawn and indebted to the bank, there is no advice than to act sensibly and pay back. There is literally no good in stressing about something that is inevitable in life except bringing more unhappiness and sorrow. To manage financial stress, a person needs to have a solid plan to live by in frugality and saving. There is no alternative way but to save and give back to the banks or try and earn more by aiming for a better-paid job or getting a second job.

These are only some of the ways that you can make positive changes in your life so that your days are not so hectic and stressed. There are other circumstances in our everyday life that makes us feel stressed and anxious.

Stress and worry

Most people believe a situation can be stressful. The truth is, stress doesn't exist outside of yourself and, therefore, no situation can be said to be stressful in itself. Yet, my guess is you experience stress on a regular basis. And probably more often than you would like to.

Stress alone is responsible for tens of thousands of deaths every year. Stress does more harm than many diseases, and leaves countless families grieving the loss of a loved one. This is why it is essential you take active steps towards reducing your stress levels.

Taking responsibility for your stress

Stress happens for various reasons and manifests in numerous situations. The traffic jam on your way to work, a business presentation, tensions with your boss, or frequent disputes with your spouse, all constitute potential sources of stress. There are two ways you can reduce stress:

By avoiding situations, you perceive as stressful, and

By becoming better at dealing with stressful situations.

We'll see how you can use these methods to reduce your stress levels.

How you can use stress to grow

Eliminating stress lightens your mood and gives you the energy, motivation, and freedom to pursue self-improvement. You need to find a way to de-stress. This may mean talking it out with a friend, taking a warm bath and watching comedy or simply taking a nature walk. Find out what works for you and include it in your schedule.

If you let stress consume your mind, it will begin to also consume your body. Stress is linked to initiating and worsening serious diseases and illnesses. If you constantly feel overwhelmed, either address the issue by making significant modifications to your schedule, workload, social circle, and surroundings. If doing so does not provide peace of mind, seriously pursue a specialist to help coach you into easing your anxiety. Sometimes it is as simple as taking a deep breath and pretending you're twenty even forty years in the future searching through your memories, at that time what would really matter to you? Sometimes you need to step back to see the big picture to allow yourself to let go of all of the minuscule, tedious, and often ridiculous tasks you force yourself to do. Sometimes it means treating yourself to something special, like a 60-minute massage, a scalp conditioning treatment, a pedicure, a new pair of shoes, or a night on the town.

To start managing your stress, first manage your overall well-being and second, use an effective coping process, which includes:

- Distinguish normal from excessive stress
- Recognize the top symptoms of stress
- Identify the stress triggers in your life
- Eliminate or manage your stress triggers
- See a therapist for extra support if needed

Chapter 4:

Master Your Emotions and Express Your Feelings Constructively

How to change your emotions?

First, let's differentiate two types of negative emotions. The first type are the negative emotions you experience spontaneously. These are the emotions that keep you alive such as the fear our ancestors felt when they encountered a saber--tooth tiger.

The second type of negative emotions are the ones you create in your mind by identifying with your thoughts. These emotions aren't necessarily triggered by external events—although they may be. These emotions tend to last longer than the first type. Here is how they work: A random thought arises. You identify with that thought. This identification creates an emotional reaction. As you keep identifying with that thought, the related emotion grows stronger until it becomes a core emotion.

Your tendency to identify with negative thoughts repeatedly is what allows them to grow stronger. The more you focus on your financial challenges, the easier it will be for related thoughts to arise in the future. The more you replay the argument with your friend in your head, the stronger the feelings of resentment will grow. Similarly, as you keep thinking of the mistake you made at work, you invite feelings of shame and intensify the situation. The point is, when you give thoughts room to exist, they spread and become major points of focus.

This simple process of identification allows seemingly inoffensive thoughts to take control of your mind. This identification with your thoughts, and more importantly, how you choose to interpret them, creates suffering in your life.

You believe the emotions are you and feel a strong need to identify with them. You may fall into the trap of believing you are your emotions. As a result, you identify heavily with them, which creates suffering.

Stop Negative Emotions

Thoughts are a normal part of the human makeup. Everyone has thoughts. These thoughts swirl in the mind, sometimes randomly, sometimes endlessly, always there, products of our environment. Thoughts are said to be that which separates humans from animals. Since humans are born with the ability to think and to reason, then humans are often known by their thoughts. Quite often, humans live their lives through the feelings thoughts give them.

Unfortunately, this can often mean that people are ruled by negative thoughts. Positive thoughts make people want to dress nicely, speak cheerfully, and basically enjoy the day they are given. But, too often, negative thoughts get in the way, wiping out any possibility of positive thoughts taking over. Negative thinking is the human being's first, and worst, the enemy. Just to clarify, there are times when negative emotions are quite appropriate. Hate is a negative emotion, but it is okay to hate cantaloupe or the color green. Anger is a negative emotion, but of course, the mom becomes angry when the child colors on the wall. Sadness is a negative emotion, but no one would recommend trying to feel joyful at a loved one's funeral.

The harmful negative emotions are not the ones that are appropriate for the time and very natural. The negative thinking that is harmful is the thinking that causes people to ruin their own day, their week, and their very lives because of thought in their head. Negative thoughts cause a distorted view of reality. Negative thoughts become the focus. Negative thoughts often lead to negative feelings. If the overwhelming thought of the day is that life is too hard to be tolerated today, that thought can show up in the body and the way it reacts. The shoulders will round, the back will curve forward. The face looks down toward the ground. Steps may become shorter and more shuffled. The whole body drags. This is what happens when negative thoughts negatively affect physical well-being. Everything becomes negative. The world is a grey and gloomy place.

Negative thoughts bring about feelings of anxiety. Anxiety, by itself, in small doses, can be a positive thing. Everyone has, at one time or another, felt anxious about something, whether it is the dark alleyway or the creepy neighbor. Mild feelings of anxiety are the body's alert signal that something might be very wrong with the situation. The feelings of anxiety that cause problems are those that grow from negative thoughts. When thoughts of 'I can't do that' become 'I can't do anything right,' that leads to anxiety. When fears of making a mistake at anything lead to stomach pains and nausea, that is anxiety. When feelings of unworthiness lead to depression and thoughts of suicide, that is anxiety.

When the mind is controlled by negative thoughts, bad things happen to the body. People who look at the world with great cynicism often suffer from the effects of dementia in later life. Having a bitter view of the world can also affect heart health. Angry people are more prone to having heart attacks and strokes, mainly because of the constant rise of blood pressure caused by anger.

Negative thoughts will never completely go away. Humans expect to fail. Unfortunately, this trait has been ingrained since birth in many people. When the influences surrounding a child speak in negative terms and never provide any type of positive reinforcement, then negativity becomes a way of life. But it does not need to stay a way of life. Nurture, the way people are raised, does not need to define one's life forever. People can change. All that is needed to bring about a good change is a bit of desire, willingness, and effort.

Keep in mind that no one ever made a successful move toward a more positive life and more positive thoughts without taking care of a few necessary details.

Conditioning your mind to experience more positive emotions

You are what you think about most of the time

To take control of your emotions, it is essential you understand the role your thoughts play in generating emotions in general. Your thoughts activate certain emotions, and these emotions, in

Thoughts and emotions determine your future

However, a thought in itself isn't enough to manifest things or circumstances. It must be fueled with an energy in the form of emotion, such as enthusiasm, excitement, passion, or happiness. For this reason, someone enthusiastic about his or her dream will achieve more than a pessimistic and unmotivated person.

Thus, one of the most important skills you can master is your ability to control your thoughts and emotions. This entails understanding what your emotions are, how they work, and what purpose they serve. Later, we'll discuss how you can use your emotions as a tool for personal growth.

Depositing positive thoughts in your mind

Confident people deposit positive thoughts in their mind each day. They celebrate their small wins and treat themselves with compassion and respect. Naturally, they expect good things to happen. On the other hand, people with low self-esteem bombard their mind with disempowering thoughts. Does it mean positive thinking is going to solve all your problems and eliminate your negative emotions once and for all? Of course, not. Thought manipulation is simply one of the tools you can use to master your emotions.

Changing your emotions by changing your environment

However, you do have control over some events. Do you have daily life situations that affect your peace of mind? What if you could do something about them?

Sometimes, to reduce negative emotions you simply need to avoid putting yourself in the situations generating them in the first place. Perhaps, you watch too much TV, which makes you miserable.

Below, I've listed some examples of activities or behaviors that may rob you of your happiness. Ask yourself whether they're contributing to your overall sense of well-being:

- Watching TV: Although watching TV can be fun, it's also a passive activity which may not contribute much to your happiness.
- Spending time on social media: Social media is convenient and it allows you to

keep in touch with your friends, but it can also be addictive. Facebook or Twitter can turn you into an addict craving the approval of others.
- Hanging out with negative people: People you hang out with have a tremendous influence on your emotional state. Positive people will lift you up and help you achieve your wildest dreams.
- Complaining and focusing on the negative: Do you constantly see the negative side of things? Do you dwell on the past? If so, how does this affect your level of happiness?
- Not finishing what you start: Leaving tasks and projects unfinished in your personal and professional life can have a detrimental effect on your mood. Unfinished business clutters your mind. Feeling overwhelmed or demotivated, is a sign you may have too many 'open loops' in your life.

How to use your emotions to grow?

Most people underestimate how useful emotions can be. They never truly realize they can use their emotions to grow.

Think of it this way. Your emotions send you a message. They tell you that your current interpretation of reality is biased. The problem is never reality, but the way you interpret it. Never forget, you have the power to find meaning and joy even in the worse situations.

Under these circumstances, nobody would have blamed him if he had remained bitter all his life. However, he overcame his challenges and today, in addition to being a successful motivational speaker, he's a happy husband and father of two.

The bottom line is, your emotions send you a message. In the same way that physical pain tells you something is wrong with your body, emotional suffering tells you something is wrong with your mind.

Note that throughout your day you often alternate between love-based behaviors and fear-based behaviors. For instance, you may be absorbed by a task that helps people and make you feel complete. In this moment, you don't need anything. Five minutes later you may imagine how proud your father will be once you finally earn a promotion.

Start noticing the underlying motivations behind your actions. As you do so, you'll begin to realize you spend a considerable amount of time trying to earn other people's approval, whether they be your colleague, your boss, your parents, or your partner. Notice this, and ask yourself what you can do to move from 'wanting to get' to 'wanting to give.'

To prevent resentment from building, it is necessary for you to reevaluate your interpretation of what happened, while confronting the situation or person you resent. After doing this, you must be willing to forgive and release your resentment.

People who end up reaching their wildest goals often do so because they are willing to leave their comfort zone. Over time, they learn to be comfortable with the uncomfortable. Picture one thing you were once afraid to do, that is now no big deal for you. For instance, I bet you were scared the first time you drove, or on your first day at work. Now, didn't you get used to it?

The truth is, people have the formidable ability to learn. The key is to grow accustomed to experiencing discomfort once in a while. By not facing your fears on a regular basis, you will greatly limit your potential for development. Staying inside your comfort zone can also erode your sense of self-esteem as, in the back of your mind, you know you're not doing what you're supposed to do.

Chapter 5:

Be The Real You and Stop Worrying About What Other People Think

Why you have to be real

Life can be tough. In a world that has certain expectations of how you should look and how you should act, you feel like you are constantly trying to fit in. You just want to be yourself, but how would the world see that? So, you try everything you can to fit into the world's standards, and you end up being something that you're not. Not only that, but you feel as though you could make a crucial mistake at any moment.

No Matter What, Be Yourself

If you're in a situation where you have no idea who you really are, now is the time to find out who that person deep down really is. When confronted with daily activities, don't put your censors on. Let what happens naturally happen. Once you let down your guard and let yourself react normally to life, you will begin to see who the real you is. Let that person out. This is one of the first ways to become more confident in yourself!

Learn to Walk Away from Worldly Expectations and Set Your Own Pace

Sometimes it feels like everyone has a script that they need to follow in order to survive. If they don't follow it, something bad will happen. That's not true. Society tries to get us to act in certain ways. However, break free from those expectations. I'm not saying go wild and do illegal things. Just don't conform to what society expects of you. You do still have to follow the rules and laws of the land, but you don't have to be expected to fit into a societal mold that everyone else seems to come out of.

Surround Yourself with Those Who Value Who You are

Believe it or not, there are people out there who will like the person you really are on the inside.

It's just a matter of letting that person show. Find those people who value you for who you are and make it a point to spend time with them. Breaking out of your shell can be difficult to do, but once people see the real you, they will value you for that. Confidence comes when you're comfortable with who you are and what you're doing in your life. Don't wear masks, be yourself!

Don't Take Criticism to Heart

Everyone is going to have an opinion of what you're doing and how you're acting. It's just the way it is. Sometimes that criticism is founded, but most times, it's a simple opinion that they want to express. Know when criticism is constructive and relevant. If you're sure that they are just trying to push their views upon you, then let that criticism go and continue to do what makes you who you are.

Realizing that you're beautiful is one of the first ways to be confident in who you are. We all have the habit of trying to fit into the world, and that makes it impossible to be who we truly are. How can we express confidence when we're hiding behind a mask? Let the real you out and learn to let people love you for who you are, not the way you want them to perceive you to be!

What Others Think is Irrelevant

Once you begin to show your confidence in who you are as a person, people are going to be eager to share their thoughts about that with you. Some of those thoughts are going to be encouraging while others might be incredibly critical. Knowing what to take to heart and what to leave behind can be difficult, especially if the opinions are from people who are close to you.

Remove the Negative from Your Life

People and their criticisms can be incredibly negative. Since they have opinions, they will do whatever they can to make the world the way that they envision it. This might mean criticizing those who they feel are weaker than themselves and that they can force change in. Learn to identify these people in your life and let your confidence shine through when you're around them. If they see that they cannot push you around with their viewpoints, they will eventually stop trying. The key is to be confident that you're doing the right thing for you and not conforming the expectations of the negative people around you.

Know the Difference Between Constructive Criticism and Harmful Criticism

There is some criticism out there that is meant to be helpful. It might be difficult to figure out what that is at times because our first reaction to criticism is to feel hurt and defensive. However, you must learn to take a step back from your initial reaction and think about whether or not the criticism was meant to help you or hurt you. Confidence is a tool that is built with time, and if you let criticism tear you down, then you won't see any progress in your life. Take what is constructive and leave all the other criticism behind you!

Not Letting Others' Comments Bother, You

Sometimes people can be unintentionally hurtful with their words. Even though they did not mean what came out of their mouths, it can still be a huge blow to your confidence. Learning to let the hurtful comments roll off of you will bring you one step closer to feeling confident in yourself and what you're doing in life. Don't allow other people to dictate who you are because they have no filters on their mouths. Simply smile and continue on your way in the manner you know is right for you!

Being Confident in Yourself

If you learn to not listen to everything others have to say to you, you will find that you are more confident on your own. Being aware of the fact that people will try to mold you to their expectations and that you might not always have the same group of people in your life is just one step toward finding out who you are and being confident in that person. Remember, you are a strong, beautiful individual and by finding your self-confidence, you can show the world much more than if you conform to society's standards!

Verbally Tell Yourself that You Can Do It and Believing You Can

Words have power. If you tell yourself that you can do it, then you will begin to believe that you can do it. During the project, you might start to feel that it's impossible, but if you continue to tell yourself that you can do it, then you can power through the task and finish it successfully. If you allow your thoughts to hinder your progress, you won't be able to accomplish what you set out to do. No matter what happens, continue to tell yourself that you can do it!

Go into the Task with Full Energy and Knowing You Will Accomplish it

Going into a task full-force can help you to get through it easier. If you go into a project with a negative attitude, you will more than likely struggle through the task the entire time, and more than likely, you won't even finish what you started successfully. By focusing your energy, along with a positive mindset, upon the task before you, you can and will get what you set out to do done. Once you see that your positive mindset helps you to achieve what you wish to accomplish, you will begin to find even more confidence in your abilities to do tasks and do them correctly.

Don't Allow Negative Thoughts to Change Your Attitude

When someone struggles with self-esteem and lacks confidence, negative thoughts will often prevent a "can-do" attitude. However, you can take control of your thoughts and push the negativity away. By expressing positive insights amid the negative thoughts, you will find that positivity will reign. Let that be the driving force in your attitude and don't allow negativity to change how you feel and what you wish to accomplish.

See it Through Until the End

Life has a way of putting obstacles in front of us. If we are already in a negative mindset, we will allow those obstacles to hinder our progress and leave the task unfinished. Even if you start to feel negative, push through until the task is complete. By seeing the finished product, you will begin to feel the confidence in yourself that you lacked while facing the struggles. Knowing that you made it through a difficult time or task is a huge boost to help you feel more fulfilled and confident in yourself and your abilities!

Attitude is a driving force in whether or not we can accomplish things on a daily basis. By evaluating your attitude towards life and its tasks, you will get a better idea about what can be affecting your self-esteem and hindering your confidence. However, if you go into each day with a "can-do" attitude, you will find that everything will become easier and you will be able to accomplish what you put your mind to.

Building Your Self-Worth

Building on and improving your self-worth is going to be a part of your self-improvement journey. Without the confidence and belief in your own self-worth, you will always find it a challenge to value yourself, love yourself or even name any positive traits that you may have. Suffering from low self-esteem and low self-worth can be one of the biggest hindrances in your life and the most debilitating reason that will be holding you back from achieving everything that you want if you do not do something about it.

Self-worth is how you value and regard yourself. It's how you view yourself in spite of what other people say or think about you. If you were being brutally honest, it's how you might describe yourself – warts and all!

Your self-worth is a deep-seated opinion and, as such, it can be hard to change. It could also be considered your ego.

If you have a high state of self-worth, you have a favorable opinion of yourself. You have faith in your abilities and consider yourself to be a good person. You accept your flaws and are happy and comfortable within your body and mind.

When you have low self-worth, life can seem like a constant state of hopelessness, despair, and misery. It can sometimes feel like an endless cycle, which is why many people often fall into depression if they do not have a way to cope. When nothing you do ever seems right, and seeking opinions from other people sometimes makes the situation even worse because it may not be what you want to hear, and it could end up impacting you negatively by making you feel even worse about yourself.

Rebuilding your self-worth is a step in the process that you must take if you want to improve yourself completely from all aspects. You need to rebuild your confidence and start reclaiming your life, living it to your fullest potential and the following practical tips are exactly what you need to get started.

Do the following to increase your self-worth. This won't happen overnight but, with practice and persistence, you will start to see that your self-worth is much greater than you realized.

Redefine success
==

Redefine success so that it relates to you, and not to the achievements of others. Celebrate your successes rather than comparing your achievements with others'.

Make your outer appearance a choice and not a yardstick
==

If you were the only person in the world, would you worry about how you look? Probably not. Instead you'd be quite happy with your appearance because you would never compare yourself to others. There would be no fat, no thin, no beautiful, no ugly, no fashion, and no pressure to look a certain way.

Stop comparing your outward appearance to others. We all look different and that's okay. How you look does not define you, and it definitely doesn't have any influence on your self-worth.

Seek role models for inspiration, and not comparison

Comparing your achievements to those of others will often lead to feelings of low self-worth. It's easy to think things like "I'll never be as clever, as rich, as thin, or as pretty as them" and feel badly about yourself as a result.

Rather than be jealous of a role models' achievements, allow their achievements to inspire you do be the best person you can be. For example, admire their work ethic rather than the money they have in the bank. Be inspired by what they do, and not what they have achieved.

Stop chasing the approval of others

Do you get upset when your witty social media post gets no likes? Do you feel happier when more people "love" your recent selfie? Do you post pictures of where you are or what you are doing to try and make your friends jealous? These are all signs that you are seeking the approval of others, and your self-worth is tied up with what other people think of you.

Rather than worry about the opinions of others, focus more on your opinion of yourself. Try NOT posting a picture of your latest outfit or haircut. If YOU like it, that's all that matters. Do things for your own gratification, and not for the opinions of people who only know you through social media.

Avoid Negative Talk Completely

In fact, just avoid anything remotely negative in general. Negativity is like an undesirable anchor that is designed to do nothing but weigh you down. Do not give into it and whenever you catch yourself in a negative thought, stop immediately because you are only going to make yourself feel worse. Make an active effort to turn your thoughts around into something positive, this is going to require some practice, but it can be done.

Make Celebrating Success a Habit

Whenever you've made an accomplishment, you should celebrate it because you did something incredible and you should be proud of it. It wouldn't be called an accomplishment if it was easy, and if you want to redeem your confidence and build your self-worth, it is time to make celebrating successes a habit. No matter how big or small your success may be, if you put in the effort and you reached a goal that you set out to do, feel proud and remind yourself of just how capable you are. Celebrate the success, feel triumphant and more importantly, feel good about yourself.

Validation Comes from Within

If you are going to constantly seek validation elsewhere, you're going to always be disappointed. Nobody or nothing is ever going to make you feel like you are a remarkable individual with something to offer and boost your confidence levels.

Stop Worrying About What Other People Think

Some people worry because they want to please everyone and take care of virtually everything. They strive for perfection in a multitude of tasks. Trying to dabble in more tasks than you are capable of handling is a sure-shot worry trigger. Your inability to deal with multiple tasks leads to nervousness and frustration.

It is crucial to remind yourself and others that there are only so many important tasks you can handle without making a mess of it. It is alright to ask others to pitch in when it comes to sharing responsibility.

You can delegate tasks or enlist the help of co-workers. This doesn't mean you do not care about work or people. It simply means you are prioritizing your work and life to make way for lesser worrying and more living. You are only taking on those tasks that you can do justice to rather than everything that clutters your mind with worry.

Set a self limit to the time spent on assisting others. Design limits based on the type of caring that causes worry. Remember, worrying doesn't fix anything. Worries should not be allowed to go past a particular point, and enforce your limit whatever it takes.

The objective is to live the best quality of life as long as you can. You are not going to drop dead if you do not eat that bowl of fruit one day or indulge in your favorite dessert. It is alright to let go sometimes. Permit yourself occasional slacking or periodic indulgences.

Worry begins with a potentially nagging thought. Maybe, a small and harmless trigger unleashes it. The tiny nagging thought creates a few more thoughts. Before you even realize what is happening, the mental storm starts brewing. It makes you think irrationally, unrealistically and in highly exaggerated proportions. You drain your physical, psychological and mental energy.

The mind is now filled with complete chaos. Worrying and negative thinking can have a profound impact on the way you think, act, feel and behave. It prevents you from leading a fulfilled and happy life. How then does one stop worrying? What are some of the most powerful techniques to lead a worry-free life? How can you stop worrying and start living? Here are some solid and action oriented tips to help you break free from the worry cycle.

When you actually do something you have been worrying about for long, you nip it forever. Many times, our worries are centered on our ability to pull off something successfully. There is an inherent fear of not being able to do something.

Pick something you have always wanted to do or do even better or start doing again. Give it your best. Remember – you do not lose anything by trying. You were as it refraining from doing it, which means you had already given up. Folks who are successful and happy are not much different from you. The only difference is they do not allow their worries, fears and negative thoughts to prevent their positive actions. Pursue something you have always wanted to pursue after weighing all options without the fear of failing. It can be about launching a start-up you have always wanted to build or learning martial arts or traveling alone. Once you start doing something you have been thinking negatively about and do just fine, it can do a world of good to your confidence.

If you do worry about what you can't control, you're going to instantly increase your anxiety by exposing yourself to a factor that's bound to sting sooner or later. You would keep yourself stagnant and immobile, unproductive.

Leave it at that and let the negative opinion be their problem, not yours. Carry yourself with high esteem and walk away from unconstructive criticisms that are coming from a place of insecurities.

You need to move on and focus on the positive, focus on your values and find comfort in knowing that you act in a way that's aligned with your belief system. And feel safe with the realization that you know where you are going, and it is where you want to go. Embrace yourself and let go of everything else.

Let Go & Moving Forward

Letting go of your past does not mean you must avoid the people or places that trigger your fear, unless your life is at risks. Facing the causes of your fear will actually strengthen you the more because you will be able to tackle those triggers and make them realize you are no longer under their grip.

You need to have a firm grip of your own life and take charge of your destiny-this is the only way you can stay on top of every situation that comes your way. Having a grip of your life means you have the reasonable confidence that you can face your challenges with little or no assistance but that does not mean you must take every risk. You need to take calculative risks where you can maximize your gains and reduce your losses.

Keep in mind that constant practice of self--confidence steps, such as mindful meditation, will help you sustain your focus and ability to resolve issues that come your way.

It doesn't matter which step you want to take first toward building your self-confidence, what matters is that you are consciously and actively indulging in the exercises until you start seeing results. Your results should motivate you to continue to indulge in self-esteem enhancement techniques, if you give up after few results, then you may end up reversing your gains.

Exercising forgiveness is a crucial part of this process. Needless to say, there will be people in your life that you might not like particularly, however that doesn't mean your relationship with them can't still be positive. Relationships tend to become toxic for one main reason—the inability to forgive someone for something they did or said that caused you pain. The idea of not forgiving someone for harming you may at first seem pretty reasonable. After all, if you constantly forgive someone who takes advantage of you or causes you harm you are only enabling them to act the same way over and over again. As sensible as this seems, it isn't exactly how things work. Forgiving someone isn't the same thing as ignoring their actions. Rather, it is removing the emotional pain and judgment from your assessment of their actions. Thus, you can forgive someone without needlessly exposing yourself to their negative actions again and again.

Chapter 6:

Build Confidence and Be Assertive Without Having to Fake It

Self-confidence is not self-esteem. A lot of people think they're one and the same. They're not.

Self-esteem focuses on whether you think you're worthy. It involves your valuation of who you are, what you're about and what you can contribute to the rest of the world. It says volumes about what you think your place is in the world.

Self-confidence, on the other hand, is an impression of trust in your abilities, your traits, your qualities as a person and your ability to judge things. In other words, it measures how comfortable you are in making decisions in the world around you. You're always making decisions.

Self-confidence is all about stepping past that fear. You no longer have to fear yourself because you can trust that when you make that call, it will work out for the best. It's not a one-time thing. This is not a fluke. It happens all the time because you trust yourself enough. It all boils down to being confident in what you can do.

When You Lack Confidence, This Is What Happens

Improving your confidence is going to be the best thing you have ever done to improve yourself. When you lack confidence in life, these are the possible situations you could find yourself in:

- **You Miss Out on Opportunities** – Low self-esteem and confidence are two counter-productive traits which will lead to inaction because you simply feel too awkward, shy, reluctant and worse, you don't believe that you can achieve success.
- **You Let Low-Self Esteem Cripple You** – When you lack confidence, that is when fear becomes bigger than anything else, and it becomes the only thing that matters. It cripples you, paralyzes you because your fear has become so strong it gets to a point where it consumes you, and you become so afraid that you eventually become incapable of doing or reacting to anything.

- **You're Unhappy** – When was the last time you saw a successful, confident person who didn't have a smile on their face or looked gloomy all the time? That is because in general, they are happier people, thanks to the confidence they have built up over time.
- **You Can't Stand Up for Yourself** – A lack of confidence will stop you from standing up for yourself in the moments when you need it most. This is because you no longer believe in yourself, and you feel unworthy. You don't have a solid footing to stand on because of your low self-esteem, and you put yourself in a position to be taken advantage of, where someone could just walk all over you because they know you will not firmly stand up for yourself or say no.
- **Stressed Is Your Middle Name** – Another thing that you will find a challenge when you lack confidence in life is the ability to adapt when situations change in an instant. When you find yourself in a position where you are going to have to think on your feet quickly and make snap decisions, you're going to end up feeling flustered and stressed because it becomes too overwhelming to a point you find it

difficult to cope. Why? Because you don't believe in yourself enough to trust your decisions, that is why.

Practical Tips to Help You Develop Confidence

To begin working on improving your confidence level, these practical tips are going to get you started in the right direction:

Toss Out Negativity One Day at A Time

When you wake up each morning, let the first thing you think about being your commitment to yourself. Set a goal to make it through the day without being negative and see how well you do. Don't stress out too much if you slip up every now and then, especially in the beginning. It may take a couple of tries, but eventually, you will get there, which is why you need to take it one day at a time.

Always Be Prepared

Confident people don't just waltz into a room and take control of the situation just like that. No, they only appear confident and in control because they have prepared for it. Being prepared is even easier if you know what kind of situation you are going to be faced with in advance. For example, if you knew you had an upcoming client meeting, or event that is going to involve mingling with a group of strangers, the more prepared you are, the better you will be able to handle it. Prepare some talking points, or do your research on the important people who will be at the meeting and what the topics of interests are so you have something to forge a connection with.

Everyone Is Better Than You

Nothing is a bigger confidence killer than thinking that everyone else is somehow always better than you. You need to stop comparing yourself to others and wishing you were more like them, a common behavior pattern which is visible on many who suffer from low self-esteem. It makes no sense to compare yourself to anyone else because you are NOT like them, and they are NOT like you. No two people will ever be the same, and thinking someone is better than you will only go to kill your self-esteem even more. If you want to start improving yourself, you are going to need to get rid of this mindset and start seeing everyone as equal.

Eliminate the Inner Critic

Do you have a little voice in your head that is constantly criticizing you, making you believe you are not good enough? That little voice is your inner critic, your own worst enemy. The difference between people who are confident and people who are still struggling to build confidence is that the former has already learned how to control their inner critic and its self-destructive nature. If you let that little voice be stronger than your belief in yourself, you are going to have a very tough time crawling out of your insecurity hole.

Building Self-Confidence

When it comes to self-improvement few things are as critical as self-confidence. Not only does self-confidence enable you to engage in the practices that develop self-improvement, but it also comes as a consequence of self-improvement. In other words, the more self-confident you are, the easier it is to improve your life, and the more you improve your life is the more self-confident you become. Subsequently, self-confidence can be seen as both the investment and the return of your efforts to become a better person.

Discover your strengths

Discovering your strengths may seem like a tricky task, especially if you feel that your life needs improving in a real and serious way. Fortunately, this process will prove far easier than you imagine. The fact of the matter is that the average person has plenty of skills, talents and strengths already at their disposal. Unfortunately, most people are unaware of just how amazing they already are. This is due to the fact that people are conditioned to compare themselves to others. Thus, when you compare yourself to a coworker who is better at a particular task or project than you are it can cause you to feel as though you lack any real ability. The more this happens the less happy you become with yourself since you constantly see yourself as less capable than those around you. Therefore, the first step is to stop comparing yourself to others and begin to observe the skill sets and qualities that separate you from those around you.

Dare to take risks

Needless to say, the more risks you take is the more likely you are to fail. While this may seem counter intuitive to developing self-confidence it actually serves a very beneficial role in the process. The truth is that the average person doesn't fear failure as such, rather they fear the impact that failing will have on their life. Thus, when you take risks and fail you discover something very important, namely that failure isn't as devastating as you imagined it would be. In fact, when you develop the ability to pick yourself up after a failure and get back in the game you will overcome your fear of failure altogether. Now you will have the knowledge that you are strong enough to survive any setback and live to fight another day. Subsequently, experiencing failure can actually be a highly effective way of developing the type of self-confidence that doesn't rely on things going well. This is the type of self-confidence that the most successful people in life possess, which enables them to achieve the levels of success that others only ever dream of.

Improve your chances of success

Another area that affects confidence is that of having enough resources. This is something that can be seen all the time in the case of people who are financially affluent. Rich people tend to have a sense of confidence when going into a venture. To the casual observer this may seem to be something that comes from having a lot of money. On the one hand this is true, however it isn't just about the money itself. The bottom line is that by having money a rich person has access to the resources they need in order to get the job done. Thus, while having more money is never a bad thing it isn't absolutely necessary for success or for building self-confidence. Instead, the key is to make sure that you have the necessary resources before embarking on a new venture. The better prepared you are, the more confident you will be. This goes hand-in-hand with doing the necessary research. Only when you take the time to discover all the things you need to achieve a goal can you give yourself the opportunity to be prepared, and thus give yourself the best chance of success.

Track your progress

If you apply this method to your personal life you will develop self-confidence in a way you never imagined possible. For starters, when you track your progress you can take the time to celebrate all of your wins. Unfortunately, as already discussed in this book, many people ignore the small victories that lead to the ultimate, final victory that they seek. Subsequently they rob themselves of the chance to recognize their abilities on a regular basis, something that is critical for maintaining motivation as well as self-confidence. However, if you take the time to celebrate even the smallest of victories it will go a long way to making you feel more self-confident in terms of the big picture. After all, if you are able to achieve the smaller goals you will ultimately be able to achieve the bigger goals as well.

Identify your weaknesses

It can be your personality trait or a physical trait. Always remember there is no such weakness that one cannot overcome. All it takes is hard work and dedication. Most people do not correctly identify their weakness and the areas that make them feel insecure of themselves and, as a result, suffer from a de-motivated attitude in their lives. Becoming self-confident helps one make better decisions in life and achieve success without any ado. It is essential that you familiarize yourself with your shortcomings. It is no good living in denial or with an escapist attitude. You can run from your demons but cannot break free until you confront them head on.

Plan out your course of action

Set aside a fixed amount of time from your daily schedule where you will single-mindedly address your concerns. If it is losing weight, then you will exercise for that period of time not concerning yourself with other mortal affairs of this life. Unless such dedication is shown, change remains a distant dream for most of us. Do not set very lofty targets for they de-motivate you from the very start. Set yourself realistic and manageable targets that you can foresee yourself achieving in a relatively short time span. Most people do not even initiate this change required to gain self-confidence.

Act upon it

Most people remain snugly wrapped up in the cocoon of their comfort zones and don't want to step out and sweat it out. It is essential to remember that you will have to endure much in order to change the way you are. It won't come to you while you are relaxing on your couch. Be it losing fat or gaining muscle, be it succeeding in an examination or in a real life relationship unless you work towards it, you will achieve nothing. Hence do not hesitate to act once having familiarized yourself with your shortcomings.

Reward yourself

Rewards are an imperative to work harder and with more dedication. Unless you reward yourself along with your journey of transformation, the journey will appear too arduous to complete. Rewards in no way mean stepping out of the line and deviating yourself from your goal but just a little token of pampering. This little reward gives you further motivation and keeps you going. This is to show that you love yourself and appreciate all the efforts that you are making in order to induce a lifestyle change.

Dress with Confidence and Assertiveness

What you choose to wear definitely alters the way you approach the world and interact with other people. If you wear something that something that you associate with powerful women, you are more likely to feel powerful and confident. What you wear does affect the mental and perceptive processes of the brain and this a proven scientific fact. Selecting a color that really brings out your best physical features or a cut of pants that accentuates your small waist, can really uplift your spirits and your confidence.

Play around with colors and find out which colors really look amazing on your and which really do nothing for your skin tone or eye color and your hair color. If you wear a color that really brings out all your best physical features, you will feel more confident from the start.

Know and understand your body shape. Dress to flatter your curves or lack thereof. Dressing in attire that really accentuates your figure can be the confidence boost you really need.

Know your strengths and use them to your advantage. Pay extra special attention to your body and really be honest about your strengths and shortcomings.

First and foremost, make sure you are completely comfortable in what you are wearing. Add your own personal flair to your outfits, one that really puts into visual aspects what you character is and who you are. Of course if you are eccentric, this may not be the route to follow for a business meeting. Tone it down a little but definitely include something that screams you in the outfit. Your clothes are the first thing people see when they meet you and they should be able to judge your personality from the start. Most important is feel comfortable and confident in how you step out into the world.

Dress appropriately for the occasion. Overdressing or under dressing for an occasion will not encourage confidence in you. Wearing inappropriate clothing can have you cowering in a corner, afraid to say anything or make your presence known for fear of ridicule. Save yourself having to endure such an event and really take careful care when selecting your outfit. You want to feel comfortable stepping out and voicing your opinions and really taking part in discussions.

Be completely sure that the outfit you have selected allows you to feel comfortable and at ease. Showing more skin than normal may leave you feeling vulnerable whereas showing less skin than normal can leave you feeling frumpy. You should always feel comfortable and confident to step out in the outfit you have selected. It really shouldn't leave you feeling anxious at all.

Allow your time a few extra minutes in the morning to get your outfit perfectly right and step out your front door glowing with confidence and that go-getter attitude you need to succeed.

How you dress says a lot about you as a person. It will give vital indicators to what your personality type is as well as pointing out your own quirky characteristics. Dressing to suit your body completely and to highlight your strengths and hide your shortcomings, will really leave you no alternative but to feel confident and comfortable and your body language will surely reflect that in your daily undertakings. Dress for the success you deserve and allow others to see in you what you know you are capable of.

Don't try to dress in a way that doesn't allow you the freedom to express yourself and your personality. On meeting you, people want to know whether you are bold and outspoken or daring and creative and your clothes are the perfect way to showcase these features.

Carry Yourself with The Confidence

Your posture and the way you approach people can either portray you as confident and a force to be dealt with or it can portray you as feeble, insignificant and without your own opinions. If you carry yourself with the outward appearance of having confidence, you will begin to feel it inwardly a well.

Walk straight up, with your shoulders pushed backwards and your head held high and let those who you are approaching know that you mean business and that you won't go down without a fight. Hunching over makes you appear weak and feeble and even shy and this is not want you want.

Take meaningful strides when you walk, shuffling along will make you appear shy or even ill. Stepping with purpose lets people know you have somewhere you are going and you are not stopping until you reach that destination.

Eye contact is extremely important and allows the person you are speaking with to realize that you have conviction for what you are saying and that you want to engage with them on the topic. Speak directly and with a purpose. Shrinking back into your shell and avoiding their eyes will lead them to believe that they are stronger and that your opinions will not stand up against theirs.

Make sure that you attend your meeting prepared and that there is no chance that your feathers will be ruffled and send you back to that squirming, uncomfortable being that you fought so hard to free. You have gained that confidence that you so deserve and you really must do everything possible to retain your composure. As time passes, you will more easily be able to take on encounters that are unexpected and still maintain your confident edge. As with everything in life, confidence is a daily battle that must be fought continuously and is always a work in progress.

Pay careful attention to your body language and stop yourself from reverting back to any of your old traits, the traits that belong to the person you once were. It is very easy to slip back into habits without a thought and in some cases it may just be done subconsciously. Things like nail biting or fidgeting, signs that you doubt yourself which the new you does not. By no means should you appear rigid or stiff and as if you are trying not to fidget but a quiet stillness is the perfect opportunity to show you authority and your confidence.

When seated, use the entire space and look comfortable. Sitting on the edge of the seat or crunching up in a corner are not signs of your confidence but rather a lack of. If you sit comfortably and fill your space, your presence will be known.

Hiding your hands out of sight out of nervousness can portray dishonesty so keep those hands visible, loosely on your lap or even on your hips will do.

It is often easier to get your message across when you use hand gestures along with your verbal presentation. Keep the gestures open and it will give your hands something to do besides fidget.

Important points should be accompanied by the steepling of your hands in front of you on the table. Using this gesture shows authority and a great deal of confidence.

Keep your feet firmly on the ground. The tendency is to cross your legs but this projects a negative vibe, as does crossing your arms. Besides the negative vibe, it also portrays a lack of interest in what is being discussed. When standing, use a wide stance and allow yourself to exude stability.

An easy, unforced smile is a wonderful way of opening the doors to discussion. A smile is friendly and invites the other party into the discussion with ease. A smile also shows that you are confident in your approach.

Before any planned encounter, prepare yourself, body and mind. Perhaps some light meditation and a little exercise to relieve tension and help you to keep calm and relaxed. If you feel calm, confident and relaxed, your body language will show it.

Your body reacts without your knowledge, like a knee jerk reaction. Become more aware of mood and feelings and make a concerted effort to take control of your own reactions and body. Do whatever it takes to calm you and instill you with confidence before a planned meeting and your body will play along and exude the quiet stillness and confidence you want the other party to recognize.

Turn Self-Confidence into a Habit

So, how can you turn self-confidence into a habit? Well, first of all, you need to figure out how habits work. Habits are actually made up of three things. There is a trigger or a cue. This can be a social setting. This can be words. This can be actions taken by other people. This can actually be a lot of external signals. There are many different external signals that can work as cues.

The second part is habitual action. This does not need explaining. When you get triggered, you take this habitual action. You just feel compelled to do it. Why? Because you are looking for the third element.

The third element is when you take action, it delivers a reward. That is how you develop a habit. A lot of people smoke cigarettes right after a big meal. The trigger is the sense of fullness that they feel from their meal. This is what prompts them to whip out their pack of cigarettes and light one up. That is the habitual action. They detect the trigger, and the habitual action is they light one up. Now, what is the reward they are looking for? The reward is that the nicotine in their system constricts their blood cells so that it works with their brain chemistry to increase the sense of comfort and wellness they get from the food they just ate. That is the reward that they are looking for.

Understand that habits are always composed of these parts: cue, habitual action and reward. Confident people are able to use this system, whether consciously or unconsciously; it does not matter, to remain constantly confident.

This is why it is crucial for you to always embrace and accept any opportunity to practice self-confidence. Do not run away from these opportunities. The next time you get invited to speak in front of a crowd, jump on that opportunity. Prepare for it, and then knock it out of the park. Even if you fail, that is okay. Take the next opportunity. Challenge yourself. Keep stepping up to the challenge until you achieve victory after victory. This is how you make progress.

Chapter 7:

Improve Your Social Skills and Express Yourself

Social Skills, Why It's Important and How to Get Started with Building It

Why is everyone so focused on acquiring kick-ass social skills today? What is it about this field of social psychology that's making it a rage all over the world? Why have people suddenly become conscious about acquiring social skills and flaunting them at every given opportunity? Here's why you must aim to be a social skills pro.

<u>Building Relationships</u>

Building long lasting relationships is so vital in both your professional and personal life. You can't expect to go very far if you are unable to leverage the power of solid relationships. Relationships help you lead a more socially healthier and fulfilling life. They alleviate stress, support you and introduce you to better opportunities in life. How do some people have so many friends standing by them in their hour of need? They have carefully cultivated and nurtured these relationships with their well-trained social skills. Building strong relationships helps you develop a more wholesome life outlook.

More happiness

Getting along well with many people opens multiple job and personal opportunities for you. It allows you to explore life more variedly to give you a greater sense of happiness and fulfillment. You may land your dream job just by offering a courteous smile and striking a polite conversation with someone at your neighborhood tennis club. The world is your oyster when you possess great social skills. You may be dating the next supermodel in your city simply by being a charmer who knows how to talk and displays remarkable social skills. There's just no limit to the possibilities that can be attained by being a socially savvy individual.

Better efficiency and organization

When you have sound social skills you are less likely to waste time on destructive people who drain your energy. You know when to say no assertively and don't force yourself to spend time on interactions that aren't worth your while. There is a clear understanding of people who you want to associate with from people who don't add much value to your life. You also learn to communicate with people who do not share the same interests and viewpoints as you without offending them. Thus, you have more time and energy for constructive people and activities that make your life more organized.

Enhances confidence and self-worth

More often than not, your self-confidence and sense of self-worth will be directly proportional to the quality of your interpersonal relationships. You will automatically feel better about yourself when people connect to you, you can communicate your ideas more compellingly, and you inspire people with your words. People displaying exceptionally good communication and people skills are often high on confidence. The more articulate you are, the more people are drawn to you, which makes you feel naturally wonderful about yourself.

It makes you a good leader

People displaying highly evolved social and communication skills are often handpicked leaders due to their ability to motivate and guide people. They remain calm under tough social situations, know how to deal with a variety of personalities, can talk their way through challenging scenarios, can speak assertively and have the ability to encourage people to do their best. They have the ability to influence people with their ideas, and communicate those ideas powerfully.

Increased Confidence

When you know how to interact with and read people accurately, there is far less confusion. You know what they're trying to say to you and thus know exactly how to respond. When you can accurately decipher what body language cues people are sending, or understand them on a deeper level due to personality type, you can also accurately adjust your nonverbal signals to be appropriate for the occasion, resulting in the most positive outcome.

Increased Personal Safety

Learning how to talk to, analyze and interact with people is not only beneficial for feeling better about yourself, but it can mean the difference between protecting yourself from dangerous situations or being victimized. By being an adept communicator, you can spot red flags that can save you.

A Better Social Life

People who are socially awkward or simply don't know how to react out of shyness, are usually this way because they haven't yet learned how to both send accurate nonverbal cues and read those of other people. Maybe you're the type who likes to keep a wide circle of various acquaintances, or maybe your interest lies more in forming fewer, but deeper, bonds with people. Whatever your intentions are, learning how to analyze people will help you achieve your social goals and send the right signals to other people.

Developing Social skills

Talk less, listen more

Sometimes, we only listen to respond or think what our next lines should be. Stop this practice and listen to the person more mindfully. Listen to understand what they are saying and how they are feeling.

Avoid the urge to jump in with your two cents or cut them off before they finish speaking. Let them complete what they are speaking, and then start speaking. Few people realize that listening is probably more important in the process of communication than speaking or thinking what you are going to say next.

Avoid Drama Like the Plague

Don't treat your relationships like a soap opera or use them for personal entertainment. You are dealing with real people with real feelings. Drama never helps fix a relationship. On the contrary, it adds more chaos to it. There's more confusion, hurt and misunderstandings.

Drama can include anything from cutting off ties to calling someone names to backbiting to making person attacks. Understand that screaming and giving off ultimatums doesn't help your cause. It only makes relationships worse. Just breathe, step back for a while, take a break, and give it sometime before attempting to mend the friendship all over again. If you have to, walk away from the situation instead of building more drama.

Think About the Other Person's Mental State

At times, you may have to say something right then or you'll never be able to say it. For example, if you feel your friend has been taking advantage of you or treating you in a less than positive way, you may have to stand up for yourself without mincing your words.

You may not be able to gather the nerve to say it again. A major chunk of effective communication is what to say when. If you feel that you could have said something at a more favorable time after gathering your thoughts, ideas and arguments, put it aside for another day. You may not be in the best frame of mind when you are angry or fuming.

Take Communication Classes

Communication classes are available in many communities and are a wonderful resource for those who are looking to put their new skills to use. Communication classes are often lead by teachers, mentors, or coaches who are effectively using communication in their own lives. As a result, they can teach you how to communicate more effectively in your own life as well.

Read as Often as You Can

Reading is another wonderful way to improve your communication skills. When you read, you gain the opportunity to learn more about how other people communicate. Through this process, you can learn about many techniques and practices that are unique to various areas of communication. For example, through actively reading you can quickly pick up on what types of words are regularly used in professional writing, versus that which are used in more casual writing pieces. This will allow you to understand what type of language is typically deemed acceptable in various circumstances. It can also help broaden your vocabulary and assist you in learning how to integrate various words into unique sentence structures.

Consider Your Body Language

Our body language has the potential to contradict us in many ways, and for many reasons. As a result, we may end up inadvertently sending the wrong messages to people during our conversations. Let's explore some examples whereby your body language may result in you not effectively expressing yourself and your message to the person you are communicating with, and why these situations may happen.

Acknowledge The Other Person's Feelings

Help them deal with their feelings or emotions, whether they are directed towards you or someone else. Let them regain their balance and composure before they start expressing their feelings.

Keep Perspectives Realistic and Open

Don't place a lot of emphasis on narrow or single track thinking. Sometimes, we need to be a little flexible when it comes to accommodating other people's thoughts and feelings, without judging them. Our ability to be successful in relationships often depends on how much we are willing to broaden our thinking. Be open to discussions and stay practical.

Respect the fact that the other person can have a point of view or preference that is different from yours. That doesn't make them any less of your well-wisher or friend. It only means you both are unique individuals with minds of your own.

Do a Reality Assessment of Your Emotions?

Do a careful scrutiny of your emotions and feelings. How are feeling at the moment? What is your emotional state of mind? Are you about to say something irrational that you'll later regret? Do you really feel what you are about to say or are you simply saying it to hurt the other person? Do you have sufficient proof or arguments to back what you are saying? How did you arrive at the specific conclusion based on something someone may have said? When we don't realize we are upset or not in a very rational state of mind, things lose clarity. The mental commentary is full of unreasonable and irrational thoughts.

Communication becomes easier and more effective when you realize how you are feeling, and the impact it can have on your interaction.

Be Mindful of Your Body Language

It isn't reduced to what you say but also how you say it or the manner in which you communicate something. Everything from your gestures to posture to expressions eyes impact the message you are trying to convey. For example, when a person has a stoic expression on their face and fold their arms across their chest, you know they are speaking to you in an accusatory manner.

Convey Discomfort Without Raising Hell

You are addressing your discomfort, lowering your stress and minimizing chances of the other person getting defensive by opening the conversation in this manner. You are revealing that you care as much for the other person's feelings as you do about your need to talk but that it is important to communicate with them about the matter because you don't want it to destroy your relationship.

Learn to change how you think about yourself

Boosting your social skills effectively means that you have to change certain key elements of yourself. First, you need to learn how to change yourself image. You have a certain image to yourself. You think of yourself in certain terms. In many cases, you might not even be aware of it. You just assume these things.

You need to take a step back, slow down and clearly identify how you describe yourself to yourself. You might be shocked. There might be some surprises there. All this time you have been struggling because of the effect of this self-image that you carry with you.

Effective Communication Principles

The art of communication is essential to have for anyone to succeed in any field. People use their communication skills to convey their thoughts, feelings and emotions to others. Although all of us communicate in our own way but very few of us know how to communicate effectively. Just like everything has some principles to follow, effective communication is based on five important principles and it is not possible to excel in this skill without considering these principles.

<u>Listening</u>

Listening is very important in the effective communication as those people who are great listeners, are great communicators actually. If you have the ability to convey your thoughts and ideas in an excellent way that everyone understands and appreciates them but your listening skills are poor, your communication will not be effective at all because you will not be able to get the thoughts and ideas of others completely so, you can't respond to them appropriately. This causes frustration for the speaker and the process of communication becomes very difficult.

Effectiveness

When your communication skills are effective, you can develop good understanding with others. People you interact with will understand you, and you will understand them, and this mutual understanding is something that makes the relationships stronger and long-lasting. You won't need to use manipulation or other tactics to win the hearts of others. This will ultimately result in satisfaction with your management and they will trust you more than others.

Perceptual Filters

Sometimes people speak in certain codes and one has to be aware of them in order to pick everything correctly during the conversation. Different people have different perceptual filters that they use in communication to understand others and convey their thoughts or information.

You should pay attention to how you can learn the perceptual filters of certain people you are in interaction with, so that you can communicate with them in better way. This way there won't be any confusion and you will be able to build a healthy relationship with them.

Patience

Patience is much needed in the effective communication because it takes both time and effort to make others understand your ideas and gain the complete information and sometimes failing to do so puts you in frustration and you want to give up on your intention. At that stage, don't forget that you have to win not to lose, so just keep the positive attitude, try to find the right words to communicate your thoughts and you will ultimately succeed.

Breaking Free from the Loop of Negative Communication Patterns

Being an effective communicator and social being is also about avoiding negative communication patterns. We now know only too well how vital and indispensable effective communication and social skills are within our daily personal, business and social life.

Great communication skills aren't just needed by political leaders and orators, but anyone who desires to enjoy rewarding and fulfilling relationships. You need it for everything from negotiating a lucrative business deal to persuading your partner to dine at your favorite restaurant. Yet we falter with social and communication skills that should come naturally to us. Miscommunication leads to misunderstandings, arguments, and breakdown in relationships.

There are tons of such awkward communication scenarios where we make mistakes that break our connection with people or fail to convey a message as desired. The worst part about these communication errors is that we can't even identify where we've erred. We fail to realize why a person didn't react in the intended manner or the reason we couldn't get someone to do what we wanted them to or why they have stopped listening to us. Then, these tiny misunderstandings grow into bigger issues until you find it impossible to communicate with the other person.

Laying The Foundation for Enhanced Social Skills

Make no mistake about it. If you want to improve your people skills, you have to operate from a position of strength. You can't just fake it until you make it. For every successful impression you make, you're bound to drop the ball many times over. In fact, you might be sending mixed signals to people. However, most of the time, you seem like a fish out of the water. You fumble. You fail to get the message. Non-verbal signals fall between the cracks and you respond negatively. People can't seem to figure out who you are and what you're about.

Without self-confidence, you won't be able to consistently produce the right effect. You won't be able to communicate what you're trying to say because you're operating from a position of weakness. It comes as no surprise that socially inept people often have low self-esteem and self-confidence. These two factors go hand in hand. People who have low self-confidence operate out of fear.

Believe it or not, the more you engage in social interactions out of fear, it makes your social skill problems worse. You don't have self-esteem. You don't have self-confidence. You're just taking shots in the dark. You're crossing your fingers and hoping for the best. Last time I checked, that's not exactly a winning strategy.

You can't afford to operate out of fear. Your efforts at building up your social skills must be built on something real. It must be built on the bedrock of self-confidence. Otherwise, you probably are going to get the same results that you're getting now.

Let's get one thing clear here. Nobody is a complete and total social loser, okay? Let's get that out of the way. Even if you think you are the most socially inept person on the face of the planet, chances are you have some friends. Chances are there are some people who have a favorable impression of you. You haven't completely dropped the ball. You're not a social disaster across the board.

The reason for this, of course, is the fact that from time to time, you do manage to create a positive social connection. Everybody's capable of this. But if you truly want to enhance your social skills so you can consistently produce positive social interaction, you need to step out of this. You need to get out of the shadow of a random chance because that's what all this is. That's all you have.

Some days are better than others, but you don't really know when the next good day is going to come around. That, unfortunately, is not a winning strategy. It never was, it isn't now, and it probably will never be a winning strategy. You have to have something more consistent, predictable and stable.

The reason for this erratic results is due to the fact you often suffer from a social downward spiral. It works out in roughly this way. You have low self-esteem. Deep down, at some level or other, you feel you're not worthy. You might even think you're an impostor, a fraud, or somebody who's just trying to pass himself or herself off as somebody they're not.

Whatever the case may be, you think you are not good enough. This, of course, is not a good foundation for self-confidence. At some level or other, you feel you're just not capable. You may psyche yourself up to try, but it isn't good enough. You just don't have that level of confidence. You don't feel like whatever it is that you're about to do has a high likelihood of success. This leads to you second-guessing yourself.

This leads to you misreading the social signals being sent to you. Time and time again, this leads to bad or awkward social attempts. Your efforts at reaching out and trying to make other people comfortable and otherwise, engage in a two-way discussion is not as good as it could be. In fact, in many cases, it ends up in failure. You feel awkward, weird, the person is put off or even offended. What do you think happens when that plays out? It leads to lower self-esteem on your part. You get direct evidence, at least that's how you're reading this, that you are not worthy. That there is something wrong with you.

Chapter 8:

Build Meaningful Relationships by Being Genuine and Without Needing to Fake It

Get rid of Toxic Relationships

It is rightly said that you are an average of the people you spend maximum time with. The best part is – you decide who you want to spend time with and who needs your time the most. Thankfully, technology is at your rescue to build thoughtful long distance relationships. You can message people more frequently, and enjoy greater connections.

Positive people infuse a sense of positivity in you. They give you energy, purpose, inspiration, motivation and a strong character. Negative people, on the hand, deflate your energy, make you feel emotionally drained, divert you from your goals and drive you towards worthless/self-destructive pursuits. They may come with their own underlying emotional issues or be victims of bad habits.

The less time you invest in such people, the better it will be for your thought patterns. How many times have you had people telling you that you will never be able to achieve a particular goal just because they think it is impossible? How do you feel about your goal after that? Most likely, not very positive.

Associating with such people also leaves behind a trail of toxic memories. The emotional clutter may be due to betrayal or infidelity or abuse. Memories about these folks can be associated with feelings of rage, revenge, disappointment and sadness. Such memories automatically connect relationships with negativity and negative feelings.

We close ourselves to positivity and constructive relationships in a bid to protect ourselves from the pain of the past. This is not very conducive for positive thinking. It takes a huge effort to simply forgive and move on. Here are some powerful tips to help you break free and get over toxic relationships.

Write a List

Writing a list about the things that were harmful, hurtful or unhealthy in a relationship may give you closure. It can help you get rid of the emotional baggage of the past, and move ahead with greater positivity. You might still be in love with a person who treated you badly, but writing it will give you a perspective about how things were not as perfect as you wanted them to be, and you still survived. It will help you come to terms with the negatives of the relationship that you may be overlooking for long. Finally, you will feel thankful to be out of the relationship.

Self Affirmations

Do you think people who post affirmations such as "do not forget to be awesome" or "eat glitter for breakfast and shine all day" on their bathroom doors and mirrors are crazy? Not really. They are using the power of self affirmations brilliantly to invite more positivity into their thoughts. Just reading and repeating affirmations such as "My life is all about miracles" and "I am an abundance magnet" first thing in the morning makes you feel better. It brings about an overflow of positivity and inspiration.

Once our negative feelings have been proven to be false, we should instantly move to more positive affirmations. This helps us counteract hopelessness with new beliefs and positive thoughts. Your thought tone changes from "I am not good enough to be loved" to "I am not perfect but I deserve to be loved."

Connect with Genuine and Positive People

Enlist the help of positive, inspiring and genuine people in your life. Surround yourself with people who have lived through painful relationships and come out trumps. They can inspire you and help you free yourself from the web of toxic relationships. They can also lift your spirit, help you feel better about yourself, and guide you into leading a more positive and baggage-free life.

Heal and Stay Hopeful

Practice deep breathing while telling yourself that the relationship ended for a clear reason. You were not meant to be in the relationship and that better things are coming your way. The negativity in your life was discarded to make way for more positive and fulfilling relationships. Tell yourself that the hurt, guilt, pain and confidence will heal. You will find peace, hope and fulfillment in the future if you show the strength to rise above a toxic relationship.

Keep it Drama Free

One of the best ways to break free from a toxic relationship is to keep it free from any drama. The less dramatic, manipulative, dishonest and humiliation-free you keep it; the easier it will be for you to cope with the breakup. Keep yourself free from all bullshit. Avoid pointing fingers. Keep it free from games and manipulation. Do not take digs or badmouth the other person. When needed – apologize.

Forgive Yourself

Forgive yourself for your own sanity. Start the self forgiveness process by writing everything down or speaking aloud. Tell yourself that it is alright to make mistakes, and learn appropriate lessons from them. Every failed relationship can teach you a thing or two. Be thankful for the relationship and move on. Never lose yourself in the aftermath of a damaging relationship. Rediscover yourself through your hobbies and passions. Sign up for a class or join a hobby club. Pick up something that you left behind. It can be anything from a part-time job to getting a degree certification.

Face Your Fears and Interact with People

If you are never going to face your fears, you will never overcome them for good. Similarly, if you won't start to be comfortable around people and interact with them, your anxiety is bound to return sooner or later. You have to face them and learn how to socialize for this ordeal to end for good.

Here is how to go about it:

Take Baby Steps

Facing your fears in no way implies that you need to speak in a crowd of 100 people instantly. That won't help at all and will only be detrimental to your newfound peace. The right way to go about is to act like a tortoise. Yes, you got that right: slow and steady to win the race.

Identify exactly the type of social situation that makes you perspire profusely and your mind go insane, and then set small goals regarding experiencing and enduring it. If speaking in front of people scares you, start off by being around people for a few minutes and slowly increase that duration.

Have a Supportive Buddy Around

Ask a supportive friend/loved one to assist you in all such times so if he/she sees you losing your confidence, he/she can quickly calm you down. Also, if there is a familiar face in the crowd, you are likely not to feel as nervous.

Think of the Bigger Picture

Always think of what overcoming your fears will do to you and how improving on social anxiety disorder will change your life for the better. Write down those benefits in bullet points and stick it to your bathroom mirror. Every time, after you shower, go through that list to remind yourself of what you aim to pursue to get going.

Take the Plunge

You have to take the plunge so do not wait for the perfect time to face the music; just do it. After a couple of weeks of working on the strategies discussed in the previous chapters, dive right in and go in a social situation even if it is just going out for grocery. Do it without talking to people and then treat yourself to a little present. Observe your feelings right after; you're likely to feel accomplished. You then need to slowly move on to making small talk to strangers (asking for directions is a good place to start) with time so you can get over your fears.

Manage your Social Life

We all know that we feel better with some people more than with others. Some people make us laugh, others make us annoyed. Some people are giving, others are demanding. Furthermore, the people we spend time with have a massive influence on how we feel. If we spend time with friends that treat us well and make us laugh and smile, we will not only become happier, we will also become more relaxed. On the contrary, if we spend time with demanding and annoying people, we will become more stressed and frustrated.

Furthermore, these effects are not just temporary, they're lasting. When you spend time with people who you like, you will not only be happier in the moment itself, you will also be happier in the times when you are alone or spending time with other people. Unfortunately, spending time with negative people will have the same effect in a negative way.

So, you really want to improve your social life and spend time with the right people. When you choose to spend time with the right people, you become happier and more relaxed. It will merely add a ton of life quality. But how do you know which people you should be spending time with?

By now you should know how to be mindful, which is also what you are going to use here. You have to be mindful about what kind of influence different people have on you. Ask yourself these questions: Does this person make me feel better or worse? Does this person make me laugh? Does this person annoy me? Do I feel like time is flying away when I'm with this person or do I just want to get away? Does this person inspire me? Does this person turn me into a person I don't want or like to be?

For some, it can be challenging to think about people in this way, but you owe it to yourself. You should be aware of how different people influence you and what you get out of spending time together with them. Once you know how people affect you, it's much easier to choose which ones you want to spend more time with and which you want to avoid as much as possible. However, you might still find it challenging to make the right decisions regarding your social life, so let's look at some of the principles you should use to improve your social life. First, let's look at how you can build a supporting community.

Upgrade Your Community

Everyone who has been a part of a well-functioning community, be it a club, a team, a class, or something else, knows what kind of power community holds. They know how happy it makes them to know that they always have someone to laugh with, they know how relieving it can be to know that you always have someone to talk to, and they know how inspiring it can be to have the trust of others. They also know how amazing it is to know that they can always rely on someone for support in every situation.

Choose Who You Surround Yourself With

Once you have found these people, spend as much time with them as you can and connect with them. Try to create regular arrangements and make time in your calendar to spend time with these people. These people will help relieve your stress and make you a happier and better person.

Furthermore, it can be a really good idea to focus on spending some high-quality time with your loved ones where you do something that you really like and that makes you feel relaxed and happy.

Be Part of a Community

Consider becoming part of a community, which you'll see regularly if you aren't already. This can be a sports team, a yoga class, a book club, or something else. If you like spending time with that community, it will be a great way to relieve stress and get some extra quality of life. Furthermore, being part of a community like this can be a great way to build your own community.

Invest

First, you must realize that if you really want to fix or improve your relationship, you're going to have to invest some time and energy in it. Having a fantastic relationship requires a lot of work, just like a successful career does. So, be ready to work hard for your relationship and be open to trying different things to make it work. If it becomes necessary, you might also benefit from investing in a relationship therapist. For now, we are going to look at some of the things you can do on your own to make a relationship better.

Get Support

One of the essential things in a good relationship is support from your community. If your relationship is not supported by your community, it will be much harder to make it work. If your community supports you and your partner (or partners for that matter), it will be easier.

Of course, you don't have the full power over whether your community supports your relationship. However, you can use everything in your power to make your community support your relationship. And you can build a community that supports your relationship.

If you want to make your relationship work the best it can, you want to spend time with people that support your relationship. If your relationship is not supported by your community, you will not have the same safety that a well-working relationship has.

Productive conflict

Disagreements can make or break your relationship. In most cases, they break. But you can handle them such that they even leave your bond stronger. Agree to set aside some conflict time and place. Even if you're dealing with an issue, don't result in a shouting match all over the house. Sometimes the verbal wall even goes beyond your house. Set aside a time when you're both relaxed. Let's say a Saturday afternoon. Set the place as well. Perhaps in the study room or in the backyard, since the outdoors make everything better. There you can outline all your issues, discuss them and find the way forward. This does not mean that you will always agree. But you can agree to disagree. You can choose to respect each other's opinion even when you don't agree with it.

Be Inspired

One of the best ways to improve your own relationship is to learn how others make their relationships work well. Try to think of couples that inspire you. If you can't even think of one, you should find some. Find couples that inspire you, spend time with them and earn their support. Then look at what they do to make their relationships work and try to copy that and see if it works for you. If you do this, you can build a community while improving your relationship. It's really a win-win situation. One of the best ways to get better is to learn from others. That counts for almost every aspect of life, as well as your relationship. Learn from what others do to make their relationships work and see if the same things work for your own relationship.

To build a relationship, the following pillars must be present.

Love

In your effort to rebuild trust and intimacy in your marriage, you must be aware that compliments must genuinely reflect your feelings. Relationships become dormant because couples stop looking for the value in each other. They stop thinking of the wonderful traits their partner has and genuinely admires during the early stage of marriage. This is perhaps because most couples have become so focused on other things that they forgot about the admirable traits of their spouse. Take cues on the following habits if you want a heathy and lasting relationship.

Communication

Effective communication heals and restores relationships. Should there be disputes, they are best settled when couples decide to sit down and talk things out. So how do you become an effective communicator especially in something as delicate and personal as marriage? Here are some of the ways:

It is important that you try to hear each other out even if it is not easy. The art of effective communication comes in learning how to balance the conversation. When your spouse speaks, make sure you listen. Do not rebut or contradict just yet. Wait until it signals your turn.

Talk to your spouse as intently and attentively as possible – If all married couples are like this, there will probably happier and contented couples in this world and definitely no children living in a broken family.

Commitment

Mean your vows. When you marry the person you love, you make known to your partner your promises for each other. These promises are your spoken commitment that you will love your partner no matter what. Failing on this particular area means that your marriage's foundation is not that strong because you are easily swayed by problems and conflicts. But if you mean your vows and you abide by them, there is nothing too difficult to conquer.

Always speak the language of love. When you are committed to making each other happy and feel secure, your words and actions will be evident. Speaking the language of love simply means knowing what makes your partner's eyes twinkle or his or her interest beams. When you make the effort to discover things that are important to your partner, it exhibits commitment.

Commitment should ultimately be about designing your plans and making the effort to make them come true. If you are truly committed to your spouse, he or she must be part of your plans, present, and future.

Trust

Withholding information especially if it aims to mislead in order to conceal a bad behavior spells disaster in marriage. Marital disaster materializes when one party no longer trusts the other. A partner with a history of having affairs may find it hard to rebuild trust. When trust is broken, know that it is not something that can easily be switched on when you need it on or off when you do not need it anymore. Rather, it takes many bouts of honesty before it is restored.

Honesty

When a relationship lacks honesty, you do not expect a partner that can be trusted. Honesty and trust should go together. When a couple is trying to survive an affair, it would mean a lot that they become completely frank and outspoken with each other. Concealing feelings will only result to grudges.

Intimacy

Marriage is a conditional union. There is this notion that if your partner is not able to meet your needs, you are technically married but do not know the feeling of being truly married. Marriage should comprise happy moments that even if bad times come, couples will still find a way to smile. The environment of marriage should be that of love and affection, while sex takes on a special scene.

Accept your partner for who he or she really is

When you quit holding your partner responsible for all the bad things happening in the relationship, you begin to appreciate him/her not as your foe but a partner in everything. You become an initiator in the marriage and not a reactor. Eventually, you will notice that you have been giving selflessly. You are not keeping score and genuinely loving the person without calling attention to your actions. Now is the time to shift your focus from blaming to caring and loving your spouse even more. If you do these things consistently, watch how your marriage transforms.

Chapter 9:

Truly Be Who You Want to Be and Express Yourself Authentically

How to be yourself – Embrace your faults

A mistake many people make is in believing that self-improvement is about changing who you are. While you might change certain habits and practices in your day-to-day life, the reality is that you are only enhancing your better qualities while minimizing the impact of your flaws. Many people turn to self-improvement traditions in order to escape their faults. This is usually because they are unable to deal with the guilt or shame of their past, therefore they want to turn a blind eye to the flawed part of their nature that caused their guilt and shame and focus instead on becoming a perfect person. Again, this isn't what self-improvement is about. Instead, it is about discovering your flaws and accepting them. Only then can you begin to make the changes you need to make in order to become a better version of yourself.

There is another side to accepting your faults that can go a long way to helping you to make the right choices when it comes to self-improvement. This is the side that allows you to accept your limitations and work around them rather than trying to change them altogether. For example, you might find that you are painfully shy when it comes to public speaking. While some people might be able to overcome such shyness through self-improvement techniques, others might not be so lucky. In this event, rather than trying to force yourself to become someone you aren't, namely a public speaker, you need to accept your limitations and work around them. Perhaps you can avoid public speaking by having someone else do the presentation for you. Alternatively, you can get up in front of your audience and let them know that public speaking is one of your greatest nightmares. This will allow you to engage in an activity you are uncomfortable in without holding yourself to unrealistic standards. At the end of the day no one can be proficient at everything. Thus, when you find something that is beyond your natural capabilities, recognize and accept the fact that you will always have to try harder to achieve success in that area.

Develop your strengths

Once you have discovered your faults the next step to self-acceptance is to discover your strengths. The bottom line is that just as everyone has flaws and issues, so too, they also possess specific talents and strengths. Again, self-improvement isn't about changing who you are as much as it is the process in which you develop yourself in a more positive direction. Therefore, knowing your strengths is a critical part of this process. When you discover your strengths, no matter how insignificant they may seem, you gain insight into the resources you already have at your disposal. The real trick to self-improvement is to develop your strengths first. This will give you the ability to overcome your flaws and weaknesses more quickly and more effectively as you can approach them with an increased sense of confidence and purpose.

When you discover your inherent strengths and talents you can find the techniques that best fit your inherent 'design'. By utilizing your existing strengths in your efforts to improve your life you give yourself a significant advantage, one that makes self-improvement easier and more impactful overall. Again, it's all about using the tools at your disposal, not trying to change who you are completely. Therefore, take the time to sit down and review your past successes, no matter how large or small, or how recent or long ago they may be. The important thing is to discover what you are good at and to begin building that part of your personality in order to improve your life overall.

Even if organization isn't your strength you will still be able to find something that will help you to get a head start in your journey to self-improvement. You might be prone to contemplation, in which case you could start by focusing your efforts on creating a better mindset. Alternatively, you might be a very empathic person. This strength would give you a clear advantage in the areas of creating a more forgiving state of mind as well as establishing positive relationships with other people. The simple truth is that you possess a trait or skill set that will help you to master certain techniques without much effort whatsoever. By starting with those techniques you will achieve greater levels of self-improvement in less time and with less effort than if you started with the areas that focus on your weaknesses instead.

Celebrate your uniqueness

Many people make the mistake of thinking that it is about conforming to a preset idea of the perfect person. The problem with this belief is that it causes people to dismiss any qualities that differentiate them from everyone else. This is the absolute worst thing anyone could ever do. Just as there are countless colors and shades that make the world a beautiful and amazing place, so too, it is the countless variations found within people that make humanity a rich and diverse species. If everyone became the same the world would be full of one type of person performing one type of skill set. This 'sameness' would be as boring and depressing as if the entire world suddenly turned green. Even if it was the richest, most luxurious color green it would still become boring and ugly.

Finally, remember to celebrate yourself. All too often people who pursue self-improvement take on a self-critical attitude, one that is condescending and full of remorse. No one should ever feel this way about themselves, no matter how far from their ideal they may be. Therefore, always take the time and effort to appreciate and celebrate who you are. The more you improve your life is the more you should celebrate it. Self-improvement should be a happy journey, albeit one full of challenges and struggles. That said, if you have the desire to improve then you have the strength to overcome those challenges and obstacles. The trick is to always be happy being you. Celebrate your unique qualities, and use this life to express those qualities in every way possible!

Work on Your Beliefs

Working on your beliefs is very important if you want to build self-confidence. Your past beliefs, whether inherited or acquired, will determine or guide your thoughts and actions. In order to work efficiently on your beliefs, you need to take the following steps;

- Be aware of the different parts that make up a belief.
- Gradually release the emotions attached to the beliefs.
- Learn to shift your perspective so that you can separate the truth from falsehood.
- Break those bonds you have created with your past beliefs

The first step towards detaching yourself from a believe is to examine critically the different component parts that make up such belief. For instance, if you believe you are naturally an average student, you need to look at which courses you perform poorly and the ones you perform very well, for the purpose of identifying your strength and weaknesses, then you need to identify reasons you have such beliefs in the first place-were they imposed on you or you just allow them naturally?

The second step is to release the emotions attached to such beliefs. If you normally cry because your favorite team lose, take step towards detaching yourself from such emotional outburst. Learn to calm down and replace negative reactions to certain situations, with rational ones. For instance, instead of hitting someone naturally for stepping on your shoes, you give the person a verbal warning instead of physical assault. The more you release emotions attached to beliefs, the better your quality of life.

The third step is to learn top shift your perspective so that you can identify the truth and falsehood. Your parents might have told you that all black people are evil for instance and you believe it. One of the best ways to change this perspective is actually to make friends with some black people to discover the truth. Beliefs will always have power over you until you separate lies from the truth.

Now that you can separate the truth from lies, you will find it easier to break that strong bond between you and the belief-this is the last step towards breaking the stronghold of beliefs on your life. You can break the bonds or attachment you have with a belief by learning to react slowly to its impact. Gradually reacting slowly will eventually help you get over such beliefs.

Face Your Fear

Facing your fear is the perfect way to conquer them. To be candid, you will never surmount your fears if you don't tackle them. When you follow the previous chapters, your confidence level should be high enough to handle your fear. It is normal to have a little fear but when your fear is holding you back from taking steps toward moving forward then it becomes a problem. Here are steps you need to take to conquer your fear;

Face the fear

You need to have a conversation with your inner self especially on things fear is holding you from doing. You can face your fear by comparing the advantages and the disadvantages of not facing such fear. Write down these pros and cons and if the pros outweigh the cons then you need to face the fear head-on, which means you should allow the fear pass through you but without you stopping the things you want to do.

Evaluate the risk level of the fear

Most times, fear comes when you don't have enough information on the cause of the fear.

Perhaps you are afraid of flying because you have heard about many air mishaps but statistics have shown that your chance of dying through plane crashes is 1:7 million, whereas your chances of dying due to cigarette smoking is 1: 600. If speaking in the public is your fear, you should know that there is not even a single threat, hence you must have the statistics about your fear. Always keep in mind that just because it looks scary does not mean it is always scary.

Make an action plan

One of the keys to tackling your fear is to tackle it one step at a time. A little amount of anxiety is actually good and taking a step forward until the fear and anxiety disappear will help you get over it.

Extending Acceptance and Empathy Towards Yourself

Empathy for humanity is something that goes a long way. If you agree with that, you should also accept and understand that this applies to your own self as well. You need to accept, love and embrace yourself just like you would do to a loving friend. Social anxiety does stem from the fear of being in social situations, but that itself is rooted in a lack of self-acceptance and self-love.

It is often when you do not love and accept yourself that you feel not confident, which makes you think that others too would not like you much. This distorted belief is what needs to change and here's how you can do that.

Challenge Your Misleading Thoughts

Your thoughts that mislead you into believing that you are anxious do the trick. Notice how I did not write 'negative thoughts' here because that would again be labeling your thoughts as bad. Instead of calling thoughts that trigger your anxiety as negative, it is better to refer to them as misleading thoughts because actually, what they do is to mislead you into believing that you are feeling nervous which in turn triggers your anxiety.

A good approach to tackle such thoughts is to challenge them and prove them wrong. Since you allow such thoughts to reside in your mind, they settle in and then grow their roots far and wide something which strengthens them. If only you keep them from sowing their seeds, you can dismantle the huge overgrown anxiety plant successfully.

Every time any anxiety triggering thought runs through your mind, hold on to it before it spreads like wild fire and question its authenticity. Ask yourself questions such as: Is this thought actually true? Was there a time I thought and felt differently? Have I ever been in a situation when I did not feel this way? What evidence do I have to support this theory? Is there evidence that suggests otherwise? Make sure to keep the tone of your questions positive so your mind comes up with positive answers to support them.

Your mind is designed to give you answers to questions exactly the way you ask it. So if you ask yourself, 'Why do I feel anxious?', it will give you several reasons to show you why. When you think of all the reasons that trigger your apprehensive behavior, you are likely to experience it again. However, when you ask yourself questions that suggest there is reason to prove your anxiety is just a feeling that will fade away or that there have been times when you felt confident and happier, you will get answers accordingly that will prove your anxious thoughts helping you feel better.

You need to do every time an anxious thought disturbs you so you can tackle it promptly and on time without allowing it to wreak any havoc inside your mind.

Accept Yourself

With the ability to challenge your anxious, misleading thoughts and that to stay mindful at all times, you can now easily inculcate self-acceptance. Self-acceptance refers is simply the act or habit of accepting yourself fully, deeply and wholeheartedly. You need to accept yourself the way you are if you are to stop criticizing and disparaging yourself, and embrace yourself with your flaws. Naturally, when you feel better about yourself, you can then move on to overcoming your shortcomings, including social anxiety.

Every night, before going to bed, think of your shortcomings and strengths and write them down on a journal. Tell yourself that you accept and love yourself along with all these qualities and inadequacies, and you are happy with yourself which helps you become better. Give yourself a hug and every time you feel like lamenting over your flaws and social anxiety disorder, think of your strengths and use them to feel better about yourself. Soon enough, you will start to nurture positive feelings for yourself.

Control Only What's Within Your Reach

An important aspect of loving and accepting yourself is to understand that you cannot control everything and can only focus on your own self. If you are now aware of how certain people's behaviors turn on your anxiety and you are positive it is not in your head only, it is time to control the way you behave. You cannot expect such people to change because even if they are wrong, they are the ones who decide how they should live. What you can do is distance yourself from all such people. While you need to slowly work on building enough confidence to face anyone you want, there are certain people whose presence alone is toxic for you. It is best to steer clear of such people so you do not absorb their negativity.

Embrace the Idea of Not Being Everyone's Cup of Tea

Those victimized by social anxiety disorder mostly have an urge to be liked by everyone around them. You need to slowly let go of this desire and understand that you are really not everyone's cup of tea. Even the finest of teas fail to impress certain people because they aren't really fond of tea. Similarly, you too need to stop trying hard to please everyone and become courageous enough to be disliked by some people.

Yes, you should not be unkind and mean to people, but if you aren't doing any wrong and still someone dislikes you, chin up and walk gracefully. It is perfectly okay. Just like you may not like banana whereas your friend loves it, everyone else is entitled to his/ her opinion and if someone isn't too fond of you, just detach yourself from that person and focus on your wellbeing.

Chapter 10:

Continuously Improve Yourself and Become the Best Person You Can Be

Reshaping Your Mindset

To become a better version of yourself that you know is within you somewhere, just waiting to be unleashed. You long to be just like the successful individuals that you look up to, the ones who achieve one goal after another, pursue their ambitions and live their life to the fullest. To become all of this and more, what you must now start to do is to reshape your mindset.

Is it possible to change the way that you think?

It is very possible, and more importantly, it is a necessary part of the process if you want to see visible change happening in your life. Mindset here refers to the innate beliefs that you have about yourself and the qualities that you hold.

This could be anything from your strengths, talents, intelligence, and even your personality, and the difference in backgrounds, life experiences, beliefs, and situations play a role in contributing to the kind of mindset that you currently have.

If you want to become successful, you are going to need to change your mindset to change your life. Success is not just going to fall into your lap, you are going to have to work hard to get there, all the while believing that you can succeed because this is exactly the kind of thinking that is going to make the difference. Everyone wants the secret to success, and while it is true that there could be several factors which no doubt contributes to the level of success that an individual accomplishes, there is one trait that everyone who wants to succeed must start adopting if they want to see the change they yearn for – begin building a better mindset. Make the choice today to improve your life by following these practical strategies below to start reshaping your mindset:

Manage Your Time, Manage Your Life

Finally, the mighty power of time management. Self-improvement just not just about working on enhancing certain traits and qualities which you want to improve on, but about learning how to manage your time better, so you are living your most productive life. This is where you learn to put all your new and improved traits towards making your life more efficient so you can accomplish more at the end of the day. Time is a precious and valuable thing, and if you use the time you have been given wisely, it is how you are going to succeed in all the different facets of your life.

A productive person can accomplish several things in a day. An average person accomplishes the bare minimum at best in a day. These two people are given the exact same 24-hours in a day, yet the difference between the one who succeeds and the one who is just getting by is how well they manage their time.

To put it simply, time management is defined as how well you manage to organize and plan your time in a day so you can get all the tasks that you need to do done. If you are given 8 hours in a day at work, for instance, it is up to you to divide your time and allocate your tasks accordingly to everything gets done within those 8 hours, and you do this by allocating the right amount of time to the tasks at hand based on priority.

Time management matters because it allows you to focus on what needs to be done to achieve the desired results that you want. Looking "busy" at work, for example, doesn't necessarily mean you're being effective or productive. If you have experience that feeling of rushing around all day being busy yet at the end of the day you feel like you have not accomplished much, that is because your time was not managed wisely enough to produce desirable results.

Building Motivation and stay focused on your goals

Any successful person will tell you the importance of staying focused on the goal. This makes all the difference when it comes to those long-term goals that can seem to be perpetually beyond reach. All too often people can lose sight of the rewards that await them at the finish line and begin to focus instead on the struggles they are facing.

Staying focused on the big goal, while setting smaller, more achievable goals is critical for choosing the destination that you want to arrive at. This allows you to establish the direction that will take you to where you want to be. However, the destination itself is only one side of the coin. Motivation is often treated as a form of energy that is strictly mental and emotional in nature. The more physical energy a person has, the more motivated they will be to take on the task at hand. Alternatively, the less physical energy they have is the less motivated they will be. Fortunately, there are numerous ways to maintain your levels of physical energy, thereby helping you to increase both your physical stamina as well as your sense of motivation.

Become aware of your thoughts feelings and action

The best way to become aware of your thoughts is to take a step back from them and listen to them from a distance. In other words, rather than treating them as your own thoughts imagine that they are conversations of other people. While separating yourself from your own thoughts may seem a bit strange it is very necessary in order to judge them objectively. After all, most people assume that their thoughts are accurate or correct simply because of their origin. The more trustworthy and honest a person you are, the more trustworthy and honest your thoughts must be. Unfortunately, this isn't always the case. In fact, many thoughts that go through a person's mind are the stuff of fear or unresolved emotions, making them very biased and usually very misleading. Even worse, many of the thoughts that go through a person's mind are actually input from external sources such as the opinions of other people, their hopes and fears, or the values they adhere to. This means that many of the thoughts in a person's mind are not of their own making, and thus not as trustworthy as they may at first seem to be.

Focus on the solutions rather than the problems

Any successful person will tell you that the trick to achieving success comes down to one critical factor perception. Most circumstances that anyone faces are beyond the individual's control. Unfortunately, many people struggle with this notion believing that they can control external events even though that is not how things work. The more they strive to change the circumstances beyond their control is the more frustrated, stressed and ultimately defeated they become. Alternatively, when a person accepts what they cannot control they 'roll with the punches', making choices that fit in with the circumstances they face rather than trying to make the circumstances fit in with their choices. A good example of this is the weather. No one can control whether it rains or is sunny on a particular day. Nor would any sane person believe otherwise. Instead, people look to the weather when deciding what things, they plan to do on any given day. If it rains the average person will choose to stay indoors and spend their time accordingly. If it is sunny then an individual may choose to spend their time outdoors, doing things that they wouldn't otherwise be able to do. While this seems simplistic it is in fact the very mindset that can make all the difference when it comes to living a successful life. This is the process of focusing on the solutions rather than the problems.

The main benefit of focusing on the solution rather than the problem at hand is that it allows your energies to be put to better use. Any time a person focuses on the problems they focus on the things that they cannot change. This leaves their energies unused, which is what causes stress and anxiety in the first place.

Learn the lessons failure has to offer

Failure can be a bitter pill to swallow, no matter how positive a person you might be. Unfortunately, failure is a part of life, especially when you take risks and set out to turn your dreams into reality. This isn't a reflection on your abilities, rather it is simply a statistical fact. The more you try anything, the more results you will achieve—positive and negative. When you begin to see failure as a teaching tool your mindset will start to transform in a very significant way. One thing you will begin to notice is that your fear of failure is all but eliminated. Certainly, no one ever truly desires failure, therefore there will always be a slight concern over things going well. However, this is nothing like the fear that paralyzes most people, keeping them from chasing their dreams. Once that debilitating fear of failure is removed from your mind you will find a greater sense of confidence when facing any task, project or obstacle no matter how large or overwhelming it may be. This is a vital aspect of positive thinking. Again, no one can change the circumstances around them, however when they change their perception of those circumstances it allows them to find a way to turn any seeming setback into an opportunity for even greater success.

Increase focus and mental clarity

Sometimes what keeps a person from having a positive mindset isn't the nature of the thoughts they have, rather it is the amount of thoughts they experience at any given time. The fact of the matter is that too many thoughts, even those of a good nature, can be harmful to a person's state of mind. Confusion, distraction and general mental overload can be enough to bring anyone down, creating as much negativity in their mind as the fear of failure or having low self-esteem. Therefore, the need to reduce the workload of the mind is just as important as controlling the nature of the thoughts the mind ponders. The best way to achieve this goal is to increase focus and mental clarity.

Fortunately, the methods for increasing focus and mental clarity are fairly straight forward and easy to perform. They are essentially no different than the methods used to de-clutter any physical environment or to organize a time schedule. The first step is to get rid of any excess and unnecessary thoughts as often as possible. This may be a bit tricky at first, since the average mind is accustomed to allowing any and every thought to enter at will and remain indefinitely. The trick is to recognize which thoughts are important to the moment and only allow those access to your immediate focus and concentration.

Improving Your Appearance and Physical Fitness

The second step in order to improve yourself is to confront the physical realms. The reasoning behind this is simple, corroborated by science, and well-known to every educated man, woman, and child. Yet, for the purposes of being thorough, I'll discuss them here once more.

Your physical aspect does not just govern your appearance, but how you feel about yourself, the energy which you have to pursue your goals, the strength with which you carry not only your own life but the lives of those who love you and may depend on you, and lastly—the simple matter of how long you live. The physical aspect of life governs pleasure from sex, confidence in oneself, the charm and command which you exert over others around you—the last of which has been proven to directly affect how people respond to you personally and professionally, and has even been linked to greater job opportunities and greater pay packages as compared to people who are less fit or well-groomed in their physical appearance.

So, join a gym, get yourself to a dance class, aerobics, acrobatics, yoga, absolutely anything at all which would tone you up and provide a physical outlet for your mental frustrations and help you feel better about the way you look and carry yourself.

The last part of improving yourself in the physical realms involves taking care of the way you present yourself to the world—dressing and grooming. Just because your office environment doesn't **demand** formal wear does not give you the excuse to walk around looking like a bum. This applies to times when you're at home, or even going out for a casual walk. Again, no one is asking you to wear a double-breasted suit, or an office skirt, wherever you go—but do look like you gave **some** thought to your wardrobe when you stepped out. People respond better to well-dressed individuals, whether those individuals are walking around in casuals or even beach wear.

Open yourself to more opportunities

One way in which a positive attitude increases opportunities is that when a person is eager to fulfill their dreams they spend more time looking for ways to do so. They will do more research in the area they are pursuing, which will make them better informed regarding the opportunities available and how to make use of those opportunities. While this may seem overly simplistic the fact is that the more eager you are to win the more effort you will put into playing the game. The more effort you put in, the better your results will be. That is just how life works. Therefore, rather than tapping into some long-lost mystical formula, having a positive mindset increases your chances of success simply by increasing your efforts to achieve that success. The flip side of that coin is that someone who is less confident of success will be less likely to do the extra research and exploration, believing that such efforts are little more than a waste of time. Thus, they will put less effort into their goals, resulting in fewer chances of achieving a successful outcome.

Take care of your health

Taking Better Care of Your Diet

Better health overall always starts in the gut. Your gut health is directly responsible for nearly every else in your body, from balanced hormones to proper organ function. When you are taking good care of your gut health, taking care of everything else becomes significantly easier. So how do you do that?

Proper gut health starts with a nutritious diet that is rich in everything you need to not only survive but also thrive. Eating a diet rich in color and with adequate proteins, fatty acids, and other important nutrients can support you in having stronger health in general. This means that you will begin to experience greater self-worth and greater self-esteem!

In addition to what you are eating, you should also pay attention to what you are drinking. You want to ensure that you are staying well-hydrated by drinking plenty of water throughout the day. You should avoid drinking excess alcohol or consuming too much caffeine. Keeping these two levels to a minimum will ensure that your body is functioning optimally and that it has the best chance of digesting and absorbing all of the healthy nutrients you are feeding it. Another great way to enjoy more fluids throughout the day is to make homemade juices from organic fruits and vegetables. A good, high-quality, fresh-squeezed juice is a great way to add more nutrients into your diet while keeping you hydrated.

Exercising More Frequently

Exercising is an important part of our lives that many of us tend to overlook. When we do not exercise adequately, we begin to experience the side effects of this behavior both physically and mentally. Physically, we struggle to do things that may have been easy for us at one point. Perhaps we may feel like we are not on par with our peers. It can be more of a challenge to carry things, enjoy doing activities with loved ones, or otherwise stay active and involved in others' lives when we are struggling from ill health due to lack of exercise. Low stamina and increased instances of chronic pain are just two of the many things that people with a poor exercise routine face.

Increasing your daily exercise and staying on track with a routine are great ways to increase your physical and mental health. Physically, it relieves stress from your body and helps you get back in shape. As a result, your hormone levels balance out and you begin to feel better. Your body and brain function optimally, your stress levels drop, your strong emotions dissipate in a positive way, and your capacity to face things in your day to day life increases.

Receiving Adequate Rest

The idea of rest and relaxation eludes many of us. Consequently, we are usually not sleeping enough, making it much more difficult to function at optimal capacity the next day. As nights go by with sleep missing, it adds up, causing us to be unproductive and unhappy. It really is amazing how quickly a good night's sleep can turn that all around.

The general recommendation is to get eight hours of sleep per night. That means, if you stay up binge-watching your favorite show until midnight and your alarm goes off at five in the morning, you will be grossly short on sleep. We have all been there, hitting snooze and praying that work gets canceled today. Well, it's not going to happen, so all we can do is get the sleep we require to prepare us for the day. A well-rested person will have little trouble getting out of bed and will sail through their day with less stress. That is a proven fact.

Try to sleep at least 6.5 to 8 hours a night and you'll see a big difference. Eliminate all sounds in your room or try to listen to Zen-like, soothing sounds, dim the lights, and drink a glass of cherry juice before sleeping. Take a warm shower, too, if you want—so you'd easily be able to go to sleep.

Upon waking up the next day, you'd feel like you have so much energy to do what you want, and if this happens every day, it would be so good for you and your health!

Work harder

The importance of effort when it comes to achieving your goals simply cannot be overstated. Anyone who puts in constant and committed effort will be far more likely to accomplish their goals than someone who shirks hard work in favor of being carefree and lazy. Even if you have all the resources you need to succeed, only when you take action are you able to use those resources to achieve success. Without such effort those resources will just sit their collecting dust. In this light success can be seen as the sum of an equation. Resources + effort = success. The most successful people understand this rule, and that is why they share the quality of having the highest work ethic—constantly working hard to achieve the success they are striving for. They know that you cannot win the race unless you are actually willing to run the race.

Maintain self-discipline

Whenever you observe a successful person you will notice a sense of organization, purpose and self-control. All of these things serve to make the individual seem almost larger than life, as though they are in control of the very course that life is traveling in. This image is due to the self-discipline practiced by a truly successful person. Rather than being controlled by their emotions, their surroundings or the situation at hand, a successful person maintains constant control over their thoughts, words and actions, keeping them above the emotional turmoil that causes most people to behave badly. Such self-discipline ensures that their thoughts, actions and words are of the highest quality at all times, thereby ensuring that everything they do leads to greater levels of success.

By maintaining control of their thoughts, successful people are able to create a positive mindset, one that is focused on achieving the highest levels of success possible. This prevents them from being dragged down by the fears and frustrations that keep most people from achieving their dreams. In addition to being in control of their thoughts, successful people are also in control of their emotional state of mind. This prevents them from reacting impulsively in a situation, saying or doing something that they might later regret. Not only does this level of self-discipline prevent unnecessary harm and damage, it also ensures that every word spoken, action taken and thought contemplated serves to take the individual closer to the success they are committed to achieving.

Know What's Holding You Back?

Now that you have a clear understanding of how to build on your passions to boost your self-esteem so you can become more confident, the next step is to identify things that are preventing you from taking action in the here and now. You have to ask yourself: "What's holding me back? If I know all these things to be true, why am I not taking action now?" Well, if you were to write down all your limitations, it's very easy to come up with a list. Most people can easily come up with a list.

Write all of these down and give yourself several days. After that period of time, you should have a fairly long list. In fact, if you read through this, it might even seem impossible. It might seem so restricted that you are just basically bucking against the tide that you have no chance against.

Now, here's an eye-opener; I need you to look at the list and then filter them into two categories: real limitations and imagined limitations. Real limitations are actual physical, legal, or political limitations. In other words, there's a law saying you shouldn't take action, or there's a person pointing a gun at you, saying: "If you do this, I will kill you." Or you have a disability which makes it impossible to do. That is a "real" limitation. Everything else, you need to push aside to be imagined limitations.

Believe in Yourself & Your Abilities

In life, we all have our demons to face and conquer. The hardest part is making that decision to put an end to its reign over your life. Belief in yourself and your abilities is half the battle won already and if you continue on that path, steadfast in your own ambition and belief, you will succeed and the feeling when you do will be immeasurable.

A lack of confidence is often the result of having little or no belief in your own abilities and your own worth. Often these feelings come from external sources who break you down at every opportunity they get. The more negative feedback that surrounds your activities or opinions, the less confident you will feel speaking out for fear of being belittled once again.

Realize immediately that these very people who wish to break you down and belittle you, are the ones that fear your power when you are at your most confident. They realize exactly what you are capable of or will be capable of if allowed to freely show belief in yourself. These bullies, if we may call them that, have their own feelings of inadequacy which they are projecting onto you. They pass on these negative vibes in hopes that you will not outshine them. These are their own demons to face and conquer.

The sooner you decide to let go of any negativity and to stop worrying about what others will say or do, the happier and more confident you will become. As difficult as it may seem, make a concerted effort to simply wipe the thought of others from the slate and worry only about what you want to achieve and how that makes you feel. You will find that you begin to speak out more often on subjects that you have knowledge on and you will begin to show less fear in offering your own opinions and standing behind them.

Tasks will come more easily and you will be more readily willing to take them on, secure in the knowledge that if you do fail, it doesn't matter what others say, you simply keep at it until you succeed. Your confidence will grow and your fears will decrease with every passing minute and with every completed task you will realize what great potential you actually have.

Overcoming Limiting Beliefs, Self-doubts and Fears

Limiting beliefs, self-doubt, and fear are learned responses, often based on past experiences or the things we learned from teachers, friends, mentors, and parents. These barriers have a way of being passed on. Some doubts and fears are completely unfounded and are merely the result of an over-active imagination.

Some doubts and fears stem from an inner voice that whispers and chips away at your self--confidence. The moment you hear that voice becoming discouraging, talk back to it and tell it to stop.

Make your positive inner voice stronger and louder than the negative voice. This will break the thought pattern that might otherwise lead to self-doubt. Try giving your inner voice a silly name or even a funny accent. Rob it of its power by making it seem ridiculous!

Fear and self-doubt are not uncommon. There will be many times in your past where you have suffered self-doubt or fear but acted anyway. You overcame your fears and, guess what, nothing bad happened!

Self-doubt and fear are nothing more than the thoughts that most people have whenever they step outside of their comfort zone. You've acted in spite of these barriers before, and you can do it again. Remember that, in those instances, you enjoyed a positive outcome, and there is no reason to expect anything different this time.

Allow Yourself to Celebrate Daily Wins

Your judgments produce actions. I hope that much is clear. When you perceive a situation, and you fit it into your personal narrative, you come up with a judgment. The judgment is never neutral because it has an emotional component. You are triggered to respond in an emotional way, either positively or negatively. This emotional state then triggers actions. Ultimately, your judgments produce actions. Your objective observable confidence level is an action that proceeds from an internal source. Be clear about this. When you feel confident, that is an action because you allowed your emotions to have an impact on you. You either work your sense of self-acceptance, and a sense of mastery is triggered. Be aware of the fact that your feelings of self-confidence are actions in of themselves. It may not feel like you are taking action. It may seem like all of this is just taking place in your emotions, but make no mistake about it this is an action. Why?

Kill the Negative Self-Talk

We all engage in self-talk. Do not fool yourself on thinking that you are completely silent inside. All of us engage in self-talk. You just have to allow yourself to catch yourself engaging in self-talk. You are always talking to yourself at some level of other. Now, this does not have to take the form of somebody who is loudly talking to themselves and having a conversation with themselves in a public area; it can be a silent thought.

You could be sitting with your friends in a bar, and somebody says something upsetting, and then you can just hear yourself inside doing an internal monologue of saying: Oh you know, what Jeff said actually refers to me. I am a bad person. Why did I do that? I could have treated that person well, but instead I chose to act like a jerk, and on and on it goes.

There is this inner monologue that is triggered by external stimuli, and you start talking yourself. Other people cannot hear, but it still takes place because you are engaged in an internal monologue. It is perfectly okay because everybody does this. In fact, according to scientific studies, people often think in a vocal way. In other words, the more they think, the further their vocal muscles get triggered. Of course, this is more acute in some people than others; however, there is a connection between our thoughts and our vocal cords. It is as if we are trying to voice out our thoughts. This happens by default.

Program Yourself to Become Successful

We all are looking for that mental edge when it comes to achieving what we want. Most often your own mind is your worst enemy when it comes to succeeding in life. You should realize that instead of fighting with your mind you can actually program it to work in your endeavor to succeed.

Success is a powerful word, which we all realize is difficult to achieve. It takes something extraordinary to reach your goals but it is still very possible. Alongside a little dedication, programming the human mind to succeed is all it takes. Once having made your mind your best ally in the quest to succeed there is nothing that can stop you from achieving your dreams.

Learn to Say "No"

Saying no can be much harder than most of us like to admit. Truth be told, turning down other individuals your identity used to stating yes to can be unnerving and even agonizing some of the time. Is amazing what number of individuals are loaded with nervousness at the prospect of turning somebody down with certainty. This inclination generally comes when we put more accentuation on what other individuals are feeling and not on what we are personally experiencing. In any case, this is simply the inverse love. In the event that we don't say no to anything then we will overload ourselves, and that prompts unwanted feelings.

Identifying your Values & Enforcing them

Your values are important to your self-confidence and esteem. When your life is in sync with your values, you will feel happier, more content, and fulfilled.

If your life does not reflect your values, you will feel unsettled and frustrated, undermining your self-confidence in the process. Your values can also help you make decisions and choices, often affecting your physical, emotional and psychological wellbeing.

A lot of people are unaware of what their values are. Subsequently, they go through much of their lives lacking direction and meaning.

You may also notice that there are overlaps from one list to the next. That's perfectly fine – something that makes you proud could also be something that makes you happy or fulfilled. In fact, items that appear in more than one list are "hot ticket items" that should definitely make it to your core values list.

It's also okay to combine similar values to create a "super value" so if working out makes you feel happy and you are proud of your fitness, these two items could be listed together.

Now, here comes the hardest part of this exercise! Take the items on your list and put them in order of priority. This may take a few tries, and you may find your values change order according to how you feel at that particular moment. Use Post-it notes so you can reorder your values without having to keep rewriting them.

If you find yourself stuck trying to decide between two or more values, ask yourself, if you could only choose one, which one would it be? That's the one that should be higher on your list.

Continue this process until you have a definitive list.

Enforce your values with this final exercise. This will ensure your values are a good fit with your life and your vision for the future. This may be done the day after you compiled your list of values so that you can review them with fresh eyes and a clear mind.

Now you have prioritized your values, you'll clearly see what is important to you in your life, what you should be working toward, and the choices you need to make.

Living with gratitude

Expressing gratitude is one of the best ways to boost positivity. When we shift our focus from what we lack to what we possess, we operate from a more positive space. We direct our thoughts towards a more positive realm of consciousness. Being thankful for the gifts we have releases us from the pent up negativity that we tend to hold on to. Gratitude immediately instills a greater feeling of encouragement and love. When love, gratefulness and positivity reside in your mind, it is tough to accommodate negative thoughts.

The advantages of leading a life of gratitude are endless. Individuals who practice gratitude consistently by appreciating and reflecting on the things they are truly thankful for experience far more positive emotions, feel more energetic and alive, sleep much better, demonstrate greater compassion and hold on – even boast of a healthier body.

Gratitude needs not be expressed only for memorable occasions. You can be as thankful about your apple pie as your momentous promotion. Gratitude expressed for the small things in life is what makes the difference. Research by psychologist Robert Emmons concludes that simply maintaining a gratitude journal and writing reflections of gratitude consistently in it boosts our life satisfaction and overall well-being.

How can you develop a feeling of gratefulness? How can you practice gratitude in your daily life? What are the simple yet effective things that you can do to transform a state of depravity to one of gratitude and thankfulness? Here are some powerful strategies for living a gratitude filled life.

Keep a gratitude journal to list all the things you are thankful for in your life. Get into the habit of jotting down the best things that happened to you during the day at the end of the day. Alternatively, you can make a list about everything in your life that you are thankful for.

Resist procrastination at all costs

Procrastination is the enemy of self-discipline, and of success. If you're a chronic procrastinator, you might believe that you're simply a lazy person. In fact, chronic procrastination might be the very habit that caused you to seek out advice on building self-discipline. You may be relieved to learn that procrastination isn't a sign of laziness and is instead a combination of many complex drivers that cause us to delay taking action. The good news is, once you understand what's keeping you stuck in procrastination mode, you'll be able to shake it off more easily.

One of the most common reasons for fear-related procrastination is a fear of failure. It's also one of the easier types of procrastination-inducing fear to recognize. It's actually very common to procrastinate when you are not confident that you can succeed. You may be worried about not completing the task to the right standard. You may even be afraid that failing at this task may cause people to have a negative opinion of you.

Giving in to this kind of fear-driven procrastination means that you will never be able to complete anything of any great importance. Or it may cause you to delay taking action until the very last minute, meaning that ironically, you're more likely to fail.

If you find yourself in this situation, try sitting down and making a list of all the reasons you **are** likely to succeed. You should also make sure that your plan to achieve your goal is broken down into manageable steps. This will allow you to assess your progress regularly and adjust if you need to, in order to meet the end goal.

Instead of viewing all failure as a hindrance, try embracing it as a necessary step to success. If you can reframe failure as a vital part of the process of succeeding it will help you overcome fearing it.

Remember that not doing something is the biggest failure there is. If you do it and it's not perfect, then at the very worst you'll have learned something. In most cases, you'll simply be closer to eventual success. Very few people experience lives without any failures, and it could be said that our lives are eventually all the richer for the failures that we do overcome.

This fear can be harder to spot. It doesn't seem to make sense that success could be something that causes fear. It can take a lot of self-awareness to identify and combat this form of fear-driven procrastination. Often the fear of success is tied to how others might react to that success. Most of us are comfortable with the relationships we have and want to keep them. If achieving your goals makes others view you differently., and changes your relationship with them, it can be a scary thought.

One of the best ways to avoid success in life is by procrastinating. Many people are plagued by this ongoing condition that hampers them in so many aspects of their lives, some are chronic procrastinators while others only procrastinate doing those things that may cause them to be uncomfortable or that takes them out of their comfort zone. Either way, procrastinations is a sure-fire way to sabotage yourself and your chance at succeeding in life.

By procrastinating you are actually placing obstacles in your own path, you are keeping yourself from seeing yourself as a success. When you put things off you tend to feel defeated, if only unconsciously. You might as well be telling yourself, "I can't do it" when you tell yourself "I'll do it later". You are basically making an excuse to avoid doing something that you need to do, and even things you want to do. Chronic procrastination evolved from years and years of practicing this self-defeating mental attitude.

Understanding why you are procrastinating is only part of the battle. Once you know what's holding you back, you need to take decisive action to stop procrastination in its tracks and get stuff done. Ultimately, overcoming procrastination is a question of self-discipline. When you find yourself procrastinating, you need to accept that is what you're doing. Then, make a decision to get on with the task you should be doing – and just do it.

Understanding why you are procrastinating can help you immensely, but don't let that in itself become a new procrastination tool! Even knowing why you're procrastinating won't help you if you don't apply the self-discipline to get the task done and overcome it.

Commit Yourself to Happiness

If you want the law of attraction to work for you, then you have to feel positive emotions. You attract things and circumstances not only through your thoughts, but also through your feelings.

So, it is important to feel good. It is important to vibrate that positive energy that will transform you into a magnet of all great things.

One way to feel good and savor the waiting is to feel good about yourself. You have to believe that anything is possible and that you are worthy of love, joy and success. When you feel good about yourself, you will feel more confident and you will feel happier.

Make a commitment to laugh every day. If you do not feel too good, all you need to do is watch funny videos on YouTube. Remember that happiness is also contagious. Sharing a few jokes with friends can go a long way.

You have to savor the waiting. Do not get disappointed if your desires are not manifested right away. You have to trust that the universe has great plans for you. Remember that you do not have to wait until you get what you want to feel happy. Happiness is a choice so choose to be happy daily.

Happy people choose to appreciate what is there. They are thankful for what is in their lives. Happiness is a choice, and you are in control!

What are you doing moment-by-moment? Are you complaining and focused on what is missing, or are you thankful for what is there? If you are unhappy, shift focus to appreciate what is there, including your partner. Unhappy people misuse selective attention and focus on loss, on what is missing. If criticized, they dwell on this. If complimented, they dismiss it and give it little attention. If this is you, shift focus, shift attention, and use your particular care to support your happiness. Appreciate what is there and dwell on successes and compliments. When you make a mistake or are criticized, take away the lesson learned and move on, don't live on it!

Like love, happiness is a choice and life is too short not to figure out how to be happy!

Conclusion

Your fate lies in your own hands. It is up to you to take control of your life, your emotions and situations presented to you and negotiate your way safely to the other side.

There is no time to hold back or to be afraid of taking that risk in case you fail. Failure is going to happen whether you like it or not but that shouldn't be something that you allow to define you or whether you decide to take risks in the future. Failure teaches you, learn what your failures have to offer, process the information and realize how you could have done it differently and you are assured that next time you will achieve the success you are after.

The objective of the book is to help you get rid of your fears, nervousness and lack of confidence to take on the world in a more self-assured and effective manner, one communication skill at a time. Communication is the master key to building solid, rewarding and lasting relationships along with impacting your chances of success in life.

Everybody is built unique and with their own personal quirks and flaws. Learn to love yourself for who you are and realize how much you have to offer to the world. Your abilities are there; you just need to take the time to seek them out without allowing all the negative or weak point get in the way. As humans we have a tendency to place too much emphasis on the negative and not enough of the positive. Don't allow your weaknesses to overshadow your brilliance hidden within. What a sad and boring world it would be if everybody was built the same, with the same abilities and capabilities and perfect in every way. We all have something to offer and that is what makes the human race such a diverse and interesting species. The trick through all of this is to learn to appreciate yourself and acknowledge your strengths and make a concerted effort to improve those abilities.

If you are someone who has a low self image, don't sit back, take control and do something today that you will thank yourself for in the future. You are the one who controls how you feel about yourself and you are the one who can change what you are not happy about. Realize what it is and do something to rectify that situation. The sooner you do, the sooner you will bloom into the wonderful, charismatic, confident individual you were put on this Earth to be.

You are your own person in every way. Don't ever allow others to make you feel less than adequate, stand your ground and let them know that you are amazing and you deserve to be treated as such. What others think of you is not your problem, it is their problem. Do what makes you happy, believe in something with conviction and stand up for it, make decisions and don't quit even in the face of failure and always walk with you head held high. You were not created to blend into the wallpaper, you were given a voice so use it wisely and let people know your opinions even if you may seem silly after the fact.

Eat a healthy diet and follow an exercise regime. Your mind and body need the stress release. Don't compare yourself to others. You are an individual and you need to realize that. Yes, watch how other more confident people approach certain situations and learn from them. Take criticisms but don't take them to heart. Process them, take what you need from them an move on.

Never compromise what you feel or believe for the sake of fitting in. We were not made to fit in but rather to stand out and you should.

Take every opportunity that comes your way and grab it with both hands, even if you fail at least you won't have regrets about what might have been. Be confident in your decisions and if they don't work out for you so be it but do it again anyway. Don't delay your progress by waiting for the perfect moment, we all know the moment will never be perfect and there will always be some kind of obstacle. The sooner you realize that you are only using this tactic out of fear of the unknown and fear of failing, the better. Embrace your fears and take the leap and you will be amazed at how exhilarated you feel.

You are your keeper and your master and you control your body, your mind and your emotions. You are the one who determines your future and how the world perceives you. Stand up and take a bow, the world is waiting.

Your thoughts and attitudes are a key factor in your overall success as a person. Once you switch your mindset and begin to know that you can accomplish anything, you will begin to see your confidence grow and you will thrive as a person.

The practical tips to improve yourself found within this book are the answers you have been searching for all this time. Unlock the power within that you never knew you had and unleash the potential to become a success.

Printed in Poland
by Amazon Fulfillment
Poland Sp. z o.o., Wrocław

50417303R00122